"This superbly written book by Debby Akerman is one that every Christian should read, for everyone is challenged by (as Debby's first chapter is titled) 'Getting a Grip on Wait.' I have seen her struggle with waiting on God personally as we prayed and waited together for years for God to bring salvation to her husband, Brad, and to transform him into the godly man he is today. This is not a book based on popular theory or untested biblical principles. This is a book that has been forged on the anvil of God's Word, made malleable in the fire of personal experience, and shaped by the hammer and tongs of life's trials. Debby has lived through the agony and glory of waiting on God and has come out triumphant on the other side. You should run, not walk, to acquire a copy of this book!"

—DR. JIM WIDEMAN, executive director/treasurer, Baptist Convention of New England

"All of us, at one time or another, find ourselves waiting for an answer from God. Sometimes it is a quick yes, other times a firm no, and then there are the times of silence. Waiting is hard for many of us, but often in the waiting God teaches us new life lessons. Debby brings a depth of understanding from her own life experiences about the challenges and the opportunities that are found during periods of waiting for God to answer. As she connects her personal stories with Scripture lessons, the truths of God's never-ending love and His promise to always be present with us shine forth."

—WANDA S. LEE, executive director, Woman's Missionary Union

"Where, other than the Word of God, can you find a single book that addresses the 'discipline of waiting'? Debby Akerman's excellent book,

Hold On, is a fresh, Bible-centered answer to this experience that awaits us all. Writing out of her life, Debby shows how a common discipline can become an uncommon delight. You will discover that waiting is the catalyst that often turns life's messes into ministries."

—TOM ELLIFF, president, International Mission Board, Southern Baptist Convention

"Wherever you are in life's journey, through Debby's book you will discover a message of hope and strength. She has woven her story and that of others with the stories of biblical figures that illustrate that God was at work and He is still at work today. She gives great insights into understanding the blessings, joy, and strength received when waiting on God and trusting His promises."

—EVELYN BLOUNT, executive director emeritus, South Carolina WMU

DEBBY AKERMAN

HOLD ON

Finding Peace and Reward
When God Has Us
Waiting on Him

BIRMINGHAM, ALABAMA

New Hope® Publishers
P. O. Box 12065
Birmingham, AL 35202-2065
NewHopeDigital.com
New Hope Publishers is a division of WMU®.

© 2013 by Debby Akerman
All rights reserved. First printing 2013.
Printed in the United States of America.

No part of this publication may be reproduced, stored in a retrieval system, or transmitted in any form or by any means—electronic, mechanical, photocopying, recording, or otherwise—without the prior written permission of the publisher.

Library of Congress Cataloging-in-Publication Data
Akerman, Debby, 1948-
  Hold on : the rewards of waiting for God's timing / Debby Akerman.
    pages cm
  ISBN 978-1-59669-390-6 (pbk.)
  1. Trust in God--Christianity. 2. Expectation (Psychology)--Religious aspects--Christianity. 3. Waiting (Philosophy) I. Title.
  BV4637.A34 2013
  241'.4--dc23

All Scripture quotations, unless otherwise indicated, are taken from the HOLY BIBLE, NEW INTERNATIONAL VERSION®. NIV®. Copyright © 1973, 1978, 1984 by Biblica. Used by permission of Zondervan. All rights reserved.

Scripture quotations marked NLT are taken from the Holy Bible, New Living Translation, copyright © 1996. Used by permission of Tyndale House Publishers, Inc., Wheaton, Illinois. All rights reserved.

Scripture quotations marked *The Message* are taken from *The Message* by Eugene H. Peterson. Copyright © 1993, 1994, 1995, 1996, 2000, 2001, 2002. Used by permission of NavPress Publishing Group.

Scripture quotations marked NKJV are taken from the New King James Version. Copyright © 1982 by Thomas Nelson, Inc. Used by permission. All rights reserved.

Scripture quotations marked KJV are taken from The Holy Bible, King James Version.

Scripture quotations marked NASB are taken from the New American Standard Bible®, Copyright © 1960, 1962, 1963, 1968, 1971, 1972, 1973, 1975, 1977, 1995 by The Lockman Foundation. Used by permission.

ISBN-10: 1-59669-390-8
ISBN-13: 978-1-59669-390-6

Cover and Interior Design: Glynese Northam

N134131 • 1013 • 3M1

DEDICATION

To the Lord, who trusted us to wait, guided us through the wait, and blessed us with renewal after the wait.

To my husband, Brad, who has encouraged me to capture the lessons learned from God in our wait by writing this book.

CONTENTS

8		*Acknowledgments*
9		*Introduction*
11	CHAPTER 1:	*Getting a Grip on Wait*
23	CHAPTER 2:	*Wisdom for the Wait*
33	CHAPTER 3:	*The Cry of Why*
43	CHAPTER 4:	*A Template for Waiting*
51	CHAPTER 5:	*A Woman for all Seasons of Wait*
61	CHAPTER 6:	*E-waiting*
67	CHAPTER 7:	*An Expectant Heart for Waiting*
77	CHAPTER 8:	*Holy Spirit Power for Waiting*
87	CHAPTER 9:	*Our Wait Is Not Your Wait*
99	CHAPTER 10:	*Prodigal Waiting*
107	CHAPTER 11:	*And in the Meantime?*
115	CHAPTER 12:	*The Way of God's Surprise*
125	CHAPTER 13:	*Battles in the Wait*
133	CHAPTER 14:	*Waiting at the Well*
143	CHAPTER 15:	*Crossroads of Wait*
153	CHAPTER 16:	*The Intensity of Wait*
161	CHAPTER 17:	*It Is Worth the Wait*
171	CHAPTER 18:	*Renewal Follows Wait*

ACKNOWLEDGMENTS

I am deeply grateful to Kimberly and Mel, Nina and Swami, Barbara, and Eiblis and Teddy, who have trusted me with their stories of waiting and shared the deep level of trust in God that grew in their hearts as they waited for God's promises.

I appreciate the encouragement I have received from my family, my prayer partners, my co-laborer Wanda Lee, the New Hope editors, and my heart-friend Gloria Stubbs.

INTRODUCTION

Waiting is one of the more difficult things God has required of me. Waiting goes against my nature as a doer and achiever. I have had some lengthy waits that dealt with health, children, and career; but the hardest wait and most God-impacted wait was experienced as God moved us south. My husband, Brad, and I heard God's direction to sell our home and move to a warmer climate. Every indicator of God's will was flashing a green light. We were certain we had heard God speak. We obediently informed friends and family of this, put our home on the market, and found the new community where we felt God taking us. One by one, we passed on our responsibilities in our church to others. We didn't know all the whys of this move, but understood the move would facilitate early retirement, for me to use my nursing in missions, and a ministry for us to do together. This would be our great adventure with God.

Then the unexpected happened. Our home did not sell. Soon we would lose the house in South Carolina we had chosen. I began to allow doubts to shadow my thoughts. The voices of friends and family echoed in my mind, *If God really wanted you to go, your house would have sold right away.* My prayertime became times of whining, *Why?* and asking, *When?* I collected worries over my decreased earnings, having resigned my full-time position to work just a few hours a week. I became obsessed with every prospective buyer looking at our home. We were tempted to do financing on our own, advised by our realtor to consider a bridge loan. Some suggested burying a religious icon in the front yard. I was adrift in a sea of uncertainty. I became alternately defensive about God's call on our life and embarrassed that we were still there. Soon prayer was reduced to begging God to sell our house. Suddenly God's Spirit reached into my heart and showed me He had chosen us to wait and He trusted us to wait, two reasons I had never considered for waiting. In that same moment the Spirit answered my question of *How do I wait?* with *My Word will show you.* I confessed my sins of doubt, fear, and pride. As His forgiving grace washed over me, the words of Psalm 37:34 pierced my heart with promise: "Wait for the LORD and keep His way, and He will exalt you to inherit the land" (NASB). He did that. We eventually did possess our promised land, but not until He taught me great lessons of waiting for Him.

Perhaps your wait is a wait for a cure from cancer, employment after losing a job, a child to be restored from rebellion, a spouse to be saved. Whatever your wait, know that the God of perfect timing has many words of promise and encouragement for you.

CHAPTER 1

GETTING A GRIP ON WAIT

WAITING GOES AGAINST the grain of today's culture. To minimize waiting, we have traded standing in bank lines for direct deposit and online banking. We drive through the car wash and drive up to the pharmacy window. With fewer than 20 items, we opt out of checkout lines with store employees and choose self-checkout at the grocery store. With Internet service and a few taps on the keyboard, we communicate with family and friends on the other side of the world. Waiting is being eliminated from the American landscape, but not from God's plans for His people.

Waiting *on* God brings to mind the wonderful times of worship and meditation we experience—times of kneeling before the Lord, presenting our joys and our sorrows, and hearing the holy hush we find only in His presence. Waiting *for* God is not so wonderful. When we know God has heard our prayer, know He has given us a promise, and then suddenly find ourselves in a "waiting for God to act" mode; the holy hush becomes the inexplicable silence of God. When we know God can easily do what is needed, a tension results that soon erodes our spiritual attitude toward

CHAPTER 1

God's sovereignty over our lives. We know God can just think it and it will happen. God can just think the answer to our prayer and it will be so! Sadly, in our human waiting for God, we spiral away from joyful living and become part of a bleak landscape of wait.

Psalm 27:14 tells us to "wait for the Lord; be strong and take heart and wait for the Lord." Allow this Scripture to redirect your thoughts from the outcome you want and the promise you have heard from God. When our focus is only on the outcome of our wait, we miss God's blessings in the wait. What blessings? I hear you, for I, too, have cried out to God, "This waiting is useless, and You can end it right now!" God broke through to me with some deep truths of Scripture, redirecting my focus with the understanding that because He is sovereign, He has the supreme right to interrupt my life at any time and in any way. Father God has the right to move His children from the brightly colored backdrops of their comfortable lives into the precarious and drab landscape of waiting. It is God who ordains our waiting time and place, just as He ordains our times and places of joy. With this realization, my journey of discovery of what Scripture tells us about waiting for God began. I took the first step to get a God-sized grip on waiting.

"Wait for the Lord." God asks us to wait. David declared this with the confidence born from personal experience. I echo these words to you. In the personal disappointment of a major time of waiting, I heard God whisper a reminder that He, my sovereign Lord, had chosen me to join Him in the wait. Not to wait alone, not to wait in silence, but to wait with Him. God spoke to my heart that He had chosen me for this wait so I would not miss any step of how He unfolds His promises. If then, our God who knows everything about us, our weaknesses and our strengths, chooses us to wait, perhaps He also trusts us to wait.

We speak often of trusting God. But have you ever thought that the reciprocal side of the "trusting in God" piece is God trusting us? What does God's trust in us look like? When I was a little girl, my dad would lie on the floor with his hands raised straight over his head, palms up. I would stand on the palms of his hands. Slowly Dad raised me into the air. There was a bit of precarious wiggling on my part, and Dad saying, "Hold real still. Get your balance. Don't look down, Debby. You are OK. I've got you." And then, once this great feat was accomplished, Dad's hands would bring me slowly back down again. I trusted my dad not to let me fall. Dad trusted me to listen to his voice, to follow his instructions, and to stand tall on the palms of his strong hands. God trusts us in the precariousness of waiting to listen to His voice, to follow His instructions, and to stand tall on the palms of His holy hands.

The Way to Wait—David's Example

If trusting us to wait, there must be a way He would have us wait for Him. Most of us equate waiting times as times of inactivity, enforced rest, or perhaps spinning our wheels while accomplishing little. Those of us who are doers resist these waiting times, seeing waiting times as wasted times. Not so, says the almighty God! His words are, "Be strong and take heart and wait for the Lord." These are words of encouragement and empowerment for the time we perceive as ineffective. King David was anointed to be king when just a 16-year-old shepherd boy. It was not until David was 30 that he was crowned king. Were those wasted years?

CHAPTER 1

Or were those preparatory years for David to become a man after God's own heart? Think back to your teenage years. What were the things you hoped for? What goals filled your dreams? Generations of teenagers have entertained thoughts of pursuing a vocation at which they would excel; from science teacher to soccer player, from song writer to social worker. As in David's young life, someone recognized their potential and helped steer them to achieve their goals. Then and now, the timeline from hopes and dreams to reality is not without times of waiting, of perceived wheel-spinning in activities thought to have little to do with their promised bright future.

What were David's hopes and dreams of the promised kingship at the tender age of 16? Were they of crowns and scepters, power and prestige, battles and victories?

In the quiet daydreams amid a field of docile sheep were his kingly thoughts interrupted by the important question, *How does a shepherd boy prepare to be king?* Perhaps David's grip on wait found in Psalm 27 is a result of his 14-year wait for God's promise to be a reality.

Reading through 1 Samuel we find the timeline of David's young years of waiting to become a king. Growing up the youngest of eight sons and simply a shepherd boy when we first meet him, David was the unlikely, unprincely future king of Israel. In chapter 16, God roused Samuel from his grief over the sin of King Saul and sent him to Jesse in Bethlehem. From among Jesse's sons was God's choice for the next king of Israel. Seven tall, handsome sons of Jesse were presented to Samuel one by one. Hearing from God that he was not to look on the outward appearance to identify His holy choice, Samuel waited for God's nod at the one He had chosen. Seven sons paraded by, yet there was no indication that any of them were God's choice. Samuel asked Jesse if these were all his sons. Hearing there was the youngest and probably smallest son out doing the least important family work, tending sheep, Samuel insisted that son be called to also be presented to him. The word of God came clearly to Samuel as young, healthy David entered the room. At God's command, Samuel stood and anointed David with oil. Scripture tells us in verse 14, "From that day on the spirit of the Lord came upon David in power." And so began the timeline of David's 14-year wait.

How did David get a grip on waiting? Did doubts plague his mind as he held in his heart the secret knowledge of God's choosing and Samuel's anointing promise to be the next king? Did David view this time as wasted when he was young, strong, and Spirit-covered, yet relegated to holding a shepherd's staff in the fields, rather than a king's scepter in a palace?

Perhaps God would have us remember that those same ignominious fields of Bethlehem where sheep grazed and lowly shepherds kept watch would one day be sung of and depicted in the birth story of David's descendant, King Jesus (Luke 2:8–12). Lowly serving and fields of wait are part of getting a grip on the staff for the journey from promise to fulfillment.

The second marker on this timeline of wait is David's selection to be a harpist for King Saul. First Samuel 16:14 (NKJV) tells us, "But the Spirit of the Lord departed from Saul, and a distressing spirit from the Lord troubled him." *The Message* tells us, "At that very moment the Spirit of God left Saul and in its place a black mood sent by God settled on him. He was terrified." Scripture goes on to say how King Saul's attendants recognized the torment as being from God. David's musical ability on the harp was

CHAPTER 1

skillful enough to have been noted and recommended to King Saul to soothe his troubled soul.

Since his anointing, God had been at work preparing David for this next step by adding to his résumé. The king's attendant recommended him with these words: "I have seen a son of Jesse of Bethlehem who knows how to play the lyre. He is a brave man and a warrior. He speaks well and is a fine-looking man. And the Lord is with him" (1 Samuel 16:17–18). This was a most interesting recommendation and one on which Saul acted. Saul asked for David, unaware that his personal need for soul soothing would provide David with a firsthand look at palace life and knowledge of how the nation of Israel was governed. In our waits for God, He is at work orchestrating the outcome and putting each person and situation in place for His promise to be fulfilled.

The next marker on David's timeline of wait was huge—Goliath! Apparently David was back and forth from serving Saul as musician and then armor bearer, to back home again as the youngest son herding the sheep. While Saul and his army went out to battle the Philistines, David was home tending sheep. His three eldest brothers were part of Saul's Israelite army. Worried about his sons, Jesse sent David to find them, give them food, and return with assurances of their well-being. You know the story. David, appalled at the defiance of Goliath against God's army, boldly stepped forward declaring he would face this adversary that had every other warrior shaking in their sandals. His brothers and the entire army saw only a shepherd boy with a slingshot. But Saul, perhaps seeing the hand of God as David declared the Lord would deliver him, sent him into battle. As every small child hearing Bible stories knows, David slew Goliath with three smooth stones, a slingshot, and the power of God's name. You can read the whole story in 1 Samuel 17.

There are giant obstacles in the journey through a landscape of wait. God has given us the weapons that best fit us for these obstacles. Like David with his slingshot, what God has given us may not look equal to facing our giants, may not be the weapons others use to fight similar battles, but the power of God's name will give us victory over any obstacle to His fulfilled promise.

If you are now thinking about your own timeline of waiting for your promise from God, maybe there is emerging the face of a friend that God has given you for waiting, so that you need not wait alone. David had such a friend. David, once beloved by King Saul as he played his soothing music, had become the object of Saul's jealousy and hatred. Along this timeline and to soothe David's troubled spirit as Saul sought to kill him, God provided a friend who became closer than his own brothers. Jonathan, son of Saul, emerged as David's heart-friend to strengthen and encourage David's relationship with God. Take time and read of this unlikely yet God-directed friendship between David and Jonathan in 1 Samuel 20.

Many peaks and valleys appeared along David's timeline. The Book of 1 Samuel unwinds like a World War II newsreel before our eyes—war banners, enemy lines, army battles, victories, and defeats. Throughout all of it was the pursuit of David by Saul with one purpose: to kill God's anointed and prevent him from being crowned as king. God did not waste these battles. Out of these defining, refining, hard waiting times for David, God sculpted the heart of a man after His own heart. David knew from intimate experience with God what it meant to be strong and take heart.

CHAPTER 1

Waiting in the Upper Room

We are not only chosen to wait, we are commanded to wait. Acts 1:4 (NASB) tells us Jesus' words of promise and of wait to His faithful few. "Gathering them together, He commanded them not to leave Jerusalem, but to wait for what the Father had promised, 'Which,' He said, 'you heard of from Me.'"

God often commanded His people to "Do this!"; "Go there!"; or "Be this." We apply these commands to our lives fairly willingly, at times passionately, as we soak up study in the Scriptures that encourage our hearts, equip our minds, and enthrall our souls. *Wait here!* is not what we expect to hear from God when we have so recently heard His voice say, *Go!*

"*Wait here!*" is not what we want to hear when we have clearly seen the hand of God pointing to a road of adventure with Him. Waiting is not in our plans and is not a topic we hope to study when a great promise is just down the road. But if you are reading this, then perhaps you, too, have heard God say, *Wait!* Be assured of this: not only has God chosen you to wait and is trusting you to wait, He has commanded you to wait.

We can learn from the disciples' experience of being commanded by the Lord to wait. They were commanded not to leave Jerusalem. The command to wait means staying in the place designated by God. Perhaps it means staying where we are physically or geographically as it did the disciples, or professionally or relationally. Each of us hears from God the place where we are to stay as we wait for His promised gift. We are tempted to leave—leave the town, the church, the job, the relationship. We are tempted to leave, thinking any movement is better than just standing and waiting. But if we leave, if we move ahead of God or fall behind God, we will not be in the place where His gift can be received. Like the Holy Spirit at Pentecost, God's gift will be given suddenly and swiftly. It will always be more than we have asked for or imagined. It will always be worth the wait. Don't miss your promised gift from God by leaving where He has commanded you to wait.

If God had a waiting room for His high and holy promise, this was it. This Acts 1 upper room where the disciples had so recently met with Jesus, this soon-to-be Pentecost room, was it. In this room were gathered the 11 remaining disciples, the women who had accompanied Jesus and the disciples from town to town, and Jesus' mother and brothers. We picture them with perplexed expressions, looking around at each other wondering who will tell them what to do now that Jesus has gone from them. Do questions echo unspoken in their minds? *What will happen next? How long will we wait? What is this promised gift?*

We can learn from these men and women three things. First, prayer is our first priority. Acts 1:14: "They all joined together constantly in prayer." Jesus had taught them to pray. Here is the first record of the disciples, of the church, praying together. Second, trust Scripture to guide you in the needs of waiting. Acts 1:20–21: "'For' said Peter, 'it is written in the book of Psalms, "May his place be deserted; let there be no one to dwell in it," and, "May another take his place of leadership." Therefore it is necessary to choose one of the men who have been with us the whole time the Lord Jesus was living among us.'" Not only was Jesus' betrayal prophesied in Scripture, but instructions were there to guide the disciples. And third, pray some more, asking God to show you what to do. Acts 1:24: Then they prayed, "Lord, you know everyone's heart. Show us."

CHAPTER 1

Because the followers of Jesus obeyed and were all in God's designated waiting place, all received the promise. We can't even imagine the pain it would have been to the heart and spirit of even one believer who broke God's trust, disobeyed the Lord, and did not wait where commanded. When the promise came, when the Holy Spirit fell on them, it was exponentially more than anyone in that remnant of Christ followers could have asked for or imagined.

Make it your desire in any landscape of wait to be exactly where God wants you to wait. It will come, and it will be more than you can imagine. Don't miss the promised gift of God.

APPLICATION:

1. In what ways have you struggled to understand being chosen to wait, trusted to wait, and even commanded to wait?

2. What possible good could there be in any wait? In your wait?

3. Create a timeline of your personal wait, present or past.

4. How is God enabling you to get a grip on waiting through David's words to be strong and take heart?

5. Apply the lessons learned in God's Pentecost waiting room to your waiting.

CHAPTER 2

WISDOM FOR THE WAIT

WHEN THE PROMISE came in Acts 2, when the Holy Spirit fell on them, it was exponentially more than anyone in that remnant of Christ followers could have asked for or imagined. The penned words of Dr. Luke give us a picture of God's stunning promise-keeping. It is a highlighted segment of Scripture's timeline. Throughout Scripture, from life's beginnings in Genesis to the vision of Christ's return in Revelation, God gave specific promises to His people, promises that required a measure of waiting. For some there were seemingly impossible long stretches of waiting for the fulfillment of the promise. All of God's children will at some time experience waiting for God.

In the beginning, as he cared for God's garden, Adam waited for a suitable life helper. He waited as every animal was required to pass by, be named by him, and assessed by God as to its suitability as Adam's helper (Genesis 2;18–20). What a zoo that must have been! Adam, who did not yet know sin existed, was perfectly patient in the wait and fully trusting in God for the perfect mate.

CHAPTER 2

When none was found, God created from Adam the woman Eve (Genesis 2:21–22). Finally, creation of all life was done, creation of man and woman. Flora and fauna were complete, perfect, and pure.

That first wait was also the only perfect wait. In Genesis 3 we learn of the fall. Satan walked into the garden as a serpent with evil feet, clearing a pathway for sin. We know the Garden of Eden story of temptation and fall into sin all too well. We can see in our mind the tree, the fruit, the serpent, and the setup for sin's entry into man. We turn the page in that story and see Adam and Eve's shame and hear God calling, "Where are you?" Out of forgiveness for Adam and Eve's sin came God's first covenant with His people, the Adamic Covenant to provide a Savior to redeem us from sin. As the sin-crafting serpent slithered out of the garden, as the first blood-shedding sacrifice for man's sin covering was made by God Himself, God's people began a more than 4,000-year wait for this promise to be fulfilled with the birth of the Savior.

Throughout that long wait were many other times of waiting for many different reasons. We can learn from all of them.

Noah, the last godly man of humankind's first 1,000 years, waited 125 years for God to storm the earth as promised. As Noah built an improbably big boat, he preached a bold message of repentance that heralded a life-ending rainstorm. Did Noah become discouraged in the wait as all who passed by rejected the repentance preached? Surely there were days he wanted to throw down his hammer and shake his fist at a cloudless sky. But then the call came! The parade of animals began as two-by-two they entered the ark. Out of God's earth-cleansing deluge rose the

Noahic Covenant and a rainbow promise in the sky. Noah's story is found in Genesis 6:9–7:24.

Only 12 chapters into the Bible we encounter the promise of God to Abram, later named Abraham, by which we know him best. At this time, Abram was 74 years old according to most Bible timelines. For 26 years, he and his wife, Sarai, who would also experience a name change, wait for the promises given in Genesis 12:2–3—promises of place, prosperity, protection, and people. God said to Abram, "I will make you into a great nation [promise of place] and I will bless you [promise of prosperity]; I will make your name great, and you will be a blessing. I will bless those who bless you, and whoever curses you I will curse [promise of protection]; and all peoples on earth will be blessed through you [promise of people]." Twenty-two years and five chapters of Genesis later, God affirmed His promise with a covenant.

This Abrahamic Covenant is one we are familiar with and have applied in countless ways in personal journeys through a landscape of waiting for the Lord. Childless women think of Sarah and apply her promise to their barren lives. Christians under verbal and physical attack for their faith apply the promise of protection to their persecuted lives. Those God has promised to use in mighty ways apply the promise of prospering in their service for God to their unrecognized efforts in kingdom work. And others are like Brad and me. When called out of our comfortable New Hampshire lives to leave family and friends, the familiar, and the fulfilling to go south without knowing the destination, we applied this promise of place and blessing.

CHAPTER 2

Keep His Way in the Wait

Psalm 37:34 (NASB): "Wait for the LORD and keep His way, and He will exalt you to inherit the land." This verse was a major affirmation of what God was doing in our lives in the early days of accepting God's call to move south, to go where He had not yet told us. With excitement we claimed this verse, or at that point the first half of this verse, as we waited for God to speed us on our way to our promised new land, as He did Abraham and Sarah.

As days turned into weeks and then months, our waiting for God lost speed and took on new, unwelcome meaning. Two months after announcing our decision to follow God's call and move, the buyers for our home disappeared. They literally disappeared, completely off the real-estate radar screen, as neither our realtor nor the buyers' realtor could locate them. They were simply gone. Many prospective home buyers viewed our home in the ensuing weeks, but not one offer was made. This did not feel like being "exalted" as our verse promised. I was discouraged and confused.

This was not my first journey through a waiting landscape with God. Since a long-ago waiting time that finally saw God's promise gloriously fulfilled, life since then had flowed with joy and peace. Prayers seemed to be answered nearly as soon as they passed my lips and were presented to the Father. Now, in this new waiting time, God gently reminded me that His timing is still perfect and His promises are forever trustworthy. Our prayers would be answered and His promises fulfilled according to His perfect plan. Thinking *perfect* meant sooner than later, we continued to wait. As the weeks again dragged by, I strayed from the path of trusting God's promise. I had to learn again the hard lesson of waiting for God.

Brad, much more patient with our wait, encouraged me to enjoy the wait and thank God that we could stay in our beautiful New Hampshire home and enjoy the remaining time there. He was confident that God's call to go had not changed and that we would go in God's timing, not ours. In spite of his loving encouragement, my morning prayertimes focused on what was not happening and what I thought should be happening. I felt the silence of a reproving, frowning God. In retrospect, my thinking is that God was silent because God could not get a word in between my daily complaints.

In an unusual moment of silence before God one morning, He spoke to my heart, *My child, I want you here a little longer.* My spirit rejoiced simply in finally hearing God talk to me. I then knew He had not forgotten us and the adventure we longed to share with Him. Spirit-empowered resilience for waiting took my heart by storm. I returned to Psalm 37 seeking new words of wisdom for our wait. The phrase "keep his way" suddenly seemed to be in bold print on the page. It was as if God was fitting my eyes with bifocals to be able to see not just the distant landscape of His promise but also the present, up-close stepping-stones of waiting. How had I missed this part? Had I not read this verse dozens of time? *The Message* presented the verse this way: "Wait passionately for GOD, don't leave the path. He'll give you your place in the sun while you watch the wicked lose it."

I refocused on these wise words for waiting: "keep his way" and "staying on the path." My desire became to wait for the Lord in ways that would please my heavenly Father. I deeply wanted our promised place in the sunny South. But more than that, in

CHAPTER 2

that moment I wanted to wait passionately by keeping God's way in our landscape of wait.

"Keep his way!" Mulling this phrase, I began to look for verses that spoke about waiting. Determining to study each one to learn how to keep God's way in waiting, I discovered waiting is indeed a major thread through the Bible.

We read in Hosea 12:6, "But you must return to your God; maintain love and justice, and wait for your God always." Second wise words for waiting—"Return to your God." How many times did the Lord God say to His people, "You must return to me"? No less than ten times in the Old Testament Scriptures I found God saying to the often unfaithful nation of Israel, "Return to me" (NIV). This return command is found in Nehemiah, Isaiah, Joel, Zechariah, Malachi, and Jeremiah. God spoke "Return to me" most often through the prophet Jeremiah, urging the people to return with all their hearts. I, too, needed to return to God with all my heart. I needed to turn from my assessment of this waiting time and return to God's ways to wait, return to God's path for waiting, and this time to trust Him with all my heart.

God authors our waiting times, already knowing how His people will wait for Him. He has seen every degree of waiting from Job's near-perfect, faithful wait for God to end his suffering, to Abraham's and Sarah's often disastrous wait to birth their God-promised child. Throughout the Old Testament, God waited for unfaithful Israel to return to Him time and time again. Israel would spiral away from godly living and into sinfulness. When in abject misery and enslavement, God would rescue them in astounding ways. Israel would, after a generation or two of faithfulness, leave the sacred altars their fathers built to God and join the revelry before the idols of pagan nations. God stood ready in

His wait to save and greet those who returned to Him. And so we are to "wait always for your God" as He has waited for us, maintaining love and justice.

Love and *justice*! Hard words to blend, but we found them applicable to God's asking us to wait. One month after reapplying the words of Psalm 37:34 to our wait, an event occurred that caused a huge hurt and great upheaval among our church family. Brad was serving as a deacon, and I was mentoring a woman caught in the middle of this crisis. God interrupted our journey with Him to keep us there where He would use us to administer His love. God trusted us to accept this delay and to embrace His interruption into our promised adventure with Him, as He brought healing and direction to our church. When the crisis abated and healing began, God continued us on the journey to sunny South Carolina with a new buyer eager to purchase our home.

There were nine extra months of waiting. Not our first nine-month wait, which was the prenatal wait for our daughter, but a much less joyous wait. This wait comingled with that of a church waiting for understanding and healing, and families waiting for forgiveness and restoration. Out of that time emerged our understanding of God's sovereign authority over His children as He interrupts our comfortable lives, calls us to venture out with Him, and to wait for His perfect timing. Only then can we understand being "exalted to possess the land."

Exalted means honored by God for keeping His ways while waiting for Him. Just as Job kept God's ways as he waited for God to release him from suffering and to restore him, we, too, can wait for God to release us from our wait and restore His promised outcome. Job received exalted restoration. "The Lord made him prosperous again and gave him twice as much as he had before"

CHAPTER 2

(Job 42:10). God always restores physically and spiritually those who wait well for Him. We may not receive the riches that Job received. We may not regain full health. We may not even be restored in this life. But God will exalt us as He moves us to possess the land of restoration, our place in the sun.

APPLICATION:

1. Identify the land God has promised to you as you wait for Him.

2. Is there a spiritual return you need to make to be able to continue to wait for God?

3. List how God is asking you to keep His ways as you wait for Him.

4. From past waits, how has God exalted you to possess the land of His promise?

CHAPTER 3

THE CRY OF WHY

THE LAND OF God's promise is beyond our reach, but it is never beyond God's reach. Because promises from God are initiated in His beautiful heart, they have had preliminary site visits by the Lord Himself. He has already traveled the roads in this landscape of wait with its hills, its detours, and its pitfalls to the promised place.

Jeremiah 29:11 gives us this often quoted promise, "'I know the plans I have for you,' declares the Lord, 'plans to prosper you and not to harm you, plans to give you hope and a future.'" When seemingly insurmountable problems arise and tilt our world, we find hope in this verse. It calls our spirits to a renewed trust in God, the Master Planner. It calls us to faithfully follow the plan He designs, a plan that will take us to a promised, prosperous future. We ask the Lord to reveal these plans. We want the never harmful, always prosperous road map for our life journeys. Like road travel of today, we want God to plug us into a spiritual GPS. We want to reach His land of promise in the quickest time and by the shortest route!

The promises we hear from God come during times of deep prayer, in the midst of dire situations. They come as we ask God for employment after job loss when the bills pile up, for healing when we are too weak for one more chemo treatment, for a glimpse of the prodigal child returning home when we can no longer bear the depravity of a young life lost in a sin-filled world, salvation for a spouse when the pain of spiritual singleness threatens to derail trust in God. What is the promise through prayer that God has spoken to you as your world tilts out of control?

Because there is nothing too hard for our God, we expect short waits for God's promises to become our reality. We expect to be hired soon, healed quickly, the prodigal returned home promptly, and the husband or wife rapidly drawn to saving faith. When the waiting time moves beyond our anticipated wait, our walk with the Lord often becomes strained. Think about your walk with the Lord as you are waiting. Are you arm in arm with the Lord striding through the unknown toward a yet unseen promise? Or perhaps for you, it is hand and hand but turning frequently to search His face for some assurance. Or, have you unlinked your arm and let go of His hand except for just a few fingertips now touching as you hesitantly, slowly go further into a darkened landscape of waiting? Some of you, with arms hanging limp at your sides, may be lagging behind the One who you thought had a plan to prosper you, not to harm you.

Journeys to God's land of promise through a landscape of wait are often slowed and even delayed by moving away from trust to apprehension, then further away from apprehension to doubt, and finally to despair. Questions that began to form in the recesses of our minds brought apprehension to our hearts. Questions gathered strength and allowed doubts to creep into our hearts. The crises that tilt our world can eventually erode trust in God and leave us in despair. It is in the pit of despair that we raise the "why" cry of our hearts. *Why me, God? Why my family, Lord? Why this? Why now? Why, God? Why?* On the floors of our homes we prostrate ourselves and pour out the whys of our hearts with wrenching sobs. Running out the door and across the yard, we race down the road to get as far from our pain and disappointment as possible. We stride out of the office and across the parking lot with rage and frustration from employment or career loss, shouting our whys to a God who promised to give us a hope and a future. We have found ourselves in a spiritual pit.

Waiting in the Pit

Jeremiah experienced many low moments in his prophetic ministry of calling God's people to repent. What hope and future did Jeremiah, who wrote these verses, find for himself when he was thrown into a cistern, into a dark, dank pit up to his shoulders in mud? This Jeremiah 38 account of impending death in a mudbottomed cistern was his lowest and most desperate moment. Here Jeremiah's real-life "in the pit" situation parallels Judah's lowest time as the battle sabers from King Nebuchadnezzar rattled and Jerusalem was about to fall to Babylon's army.

Jeremiah records his "why" cry from the pit in Lamentations 3:54–56 with these words in *The Message*: "I called out your name, O GOD, called from the bottom of the pit. You listened when I called out, 'Don't shut your ears! Get me out of here! Save me!' You came close when I called out. You said, 'It's going to be all right.'" These were not words for his own dire situation but for the fall and destruction of God's people conquered and enslaved by the Babylonians.

Jeremiah is far from alone. Scripture rings with cries of *why* to God! Some cried out from dry cisterns and others from muddy

CHAPTER 3

pits. Pits throughout the Bible were places for imprisonment or for death. Genesis tells the first pit story about Joseph. Revelation presents the prophecy of Satan's 1,000-year imprisonment. (Revelation 20). Look at a few of these pit stories.

Joseph, clad in a coat of many colors, was thrown into a cistern by his brothers (Genesis 37). Did he think God had plans to give him a hope and a future while in that cistern or was his focus on the unscalable cistern walls? The prospering of God's plan was there for the boy in the pit, but he was 30 years old before it was accomplished, before Pharaoh put his signet ring on Joseph and put him in charge of the entire realm of Egypt. A place of prominence and responsibility in Pharaoh's household was not likely to have been the substance of Joseph's boyhood dreams, but neither was it the nightmare he probably encountered as he waited for sure death in that cistern. Many years later, when Joseph was reunited with his brothers, he said with kindness: "Don't be afraid. Am I in the place of God? You intended to harm me, but God intended it for good to accomplish what is now being done, the saving of many lives. So then, don't be afraid. I will provide for you and your children" (Genesis 50:19–21).

David recalled in Psalm 40 how God lifted him out of a slimy pit, out of the mud and mire, and set his feet on a rock and gave him a firm place to stand. The life stories of David resonate often with our own stories—waiting for God's promises; long battles in life; persistent sorrow in loss; the long, slow fall into sin. These same stories inspire us with hope and help us refocus on God. They remind us of God's plan to lift us from our own slimy pits, put our feet on a solid rock, and give us a firm place to stand.

Daniel 6 tells us that because of faithful worship of the God of the Jews, Daniel was thrown into a pit with hungry lions, a sentence of horrible and certain death! King Darius had been so impressed by Daniel's dream interpretations and wall-writing analysis that he dared to hope there was some truth to Daniel's God and that Daniel might be miraculously saved. The king paced all night, and as morning broke, he rushed to see what remained of Daniel. Imagine King Darius's face when he heard not a roar from the pit but Daniel's voice saying brightly and with forgiveness, "My God knew that I was innocent, and he sent an angel to keep the lions from eating me." King Darius ordered Daniel lifted out of the pit and called for all to worship the God who miraculously saves!

We don't know what happened in the lion pit, but we know that it was not the first time Daniel had experienced God's salvation from sure death. Not once, but twice Daniel experienced the presence of God in a crisis because he kept His focus on God, not on his circumstances, and not on the wait for God to deliver him.

When we cry out to God, "Why is this happening to me again, God?" or "Why has she relapsed back into drug addictions?" or "Why is disease riddling his body again?" remember that God knows where you are on the journey, has a continuing plan for your life, and has not forsaken you in your wait for God's promise. We must replace our cry of "Why?" with a Daniel-like focus on our Father God.

CHAPTER 3

The little Book of Jonah is not only a big fish story, but a story straight from the pit of a fish's stomach. Jonah recounts his floundering in Jonah 2:2–3 (NASB), telling us "I called out of my distress to the LORD, and He answered me. I cried for help from the depth of Sheol; You heard my voice. For You had cast me into the deep, into the heart of the seas." Skillfully, the story of Jonah gives a description of that pit which reminds us of the pit of waiting we may experience as we drown in the pain, disappointments, and sorrows of long waits. But we can take hope from Jonah as he tells us, "You have brought up my life from the pit, O LORD my God. While I was fainting away, I remembered the LORD, and my prayer came to You, into Your holy temple" (Jonah 2:6–7 NASB). Like Jonah's, our prayers ascend from our own pits to the throne room of God, into the heavenly holy of holies where today, our High Priest Jesus sits at the right hand of the Father, ever interceding for us.

While we are in the landscape of waiting for the promise we have heard from God, at times situations go from bad to worse. When we have been obedient and trusted God for the promise, yet instead it seems we are on a long, slippery slope of waiting, it may feel like we are in a headlong plunge into a pit like Joseph, David, Daniel, or Jonah. As we look around, all we see are unscalable walls pressing in on all sides. Looking up, we see only a pinpoint of light above. Straining to hear a sound of rescue, our ears are filled with the sounds of roaring lions waiting to consume us. We must close our eyes and ears to all of these. We must fix our eyes on Jesus, the author and perfecter of our faith. When we have refocused on Jesus, our ears will be tuned to hear the words of Jesus saying, "I will be with your always." Our voices will call out with the words of the prophet Micah saying, "Therefore I will look to the LORD; I will wait for the God of my salvation; My God will hear me" (Micah 7:7 NKJV).

Be assured, God has no intention of leaving you to wallow in the pit of despair! Joseph, David, Daniel, and Jonah were all protected in their pit experiences. All were rescued in different ways and in ways they could not imagine. Rescue came to Joseph by a caravan of Midianite merchants on their way to Egypt. David felt the spiritual hands of God lift him in a near-physical way from despair to stand on solid, spiritual ground. Daniel once again experienced the presence of the angel of the Lord with him, saving him from imminent death. And Jonah knew what it was to be spit out on dry land at the command of our God and given a second chance to obey.

Our God has chosen us to wait for His promise. A pit of despair along our timeline of wait is not part of His plan. When God hears our "Why?" cry from pits of despair; when He hears us cry, "But LORD, be merciful to us, for we have waited for you. Be our strong arm each day and our salvation in times of trouble" (Isaiah 33:2 NLT); He rescues us to stand firm and wait for His promise with renewed patience and hope.

APPLICATION:

1. Describe in detail the promise you have heard from God.

2. Where are you in your walk toward the future God has promised?

   a. Are you striding arm in arm with God?

   b. Are you now hand in hand with much wondering?

   c. Has it become more about the why questions than fingers touching the Savior?

   d. Or, are you lagging behind the Lord on the slippery slope of despair?

3. If your wait has become a pit of despair, what are the whys you call out to God?

4. What can you do to refocus your eyes and ears on Jesus to prepare for rescue?

5. How have you experienced the strong arm of God lift you out of despair in your wait?

CHAPTER 4

A TEMPLATE FOR WAITING

*E*ACH DAY IN my biblical word study of *wait*, God revealed to me spiritual instructions that would form a template for waiting and present me with a guide for godly behavior in our waiting time. I had learned that I was chosen to wait and trusted to wait. I knew that God, hearing my cry of *Why?* from a self-dug pit of despair, had rescued me with His strong right arm. But as I was moving on with God through the landscape of wait, I didn't know what behaviors God expected from me in this journey.

Growing up in my family, equally important as seeing all A and B grades on our school report cards was seeing all 1s in the deportment columns. A's were applauded! Bs were discussed patiently with understanding by my parents. When a C arrived home on a report card, it was much more sternly addressed. I am thankful not to have discovered how Mom and Dad would have dealt with a failing grade. But I learned from experience that anything worse than a 1 in deportment resulted in dire warnings of what would happen if the 2 was not replaced by a 1 in the next marking period. I suspect my dad's zero-tolerance policy was

CHAPTER 4

in place long before that behavioral term developed for today's schools.

As I transformed that marking period's level 2 deportment into a 1, I developed into a "by the book" kind of gal. I first read and then carefully file the instruction manuals that accompany new appliances, I follow exactly the pattern directions for sewing projects, and as a nurse I adhere precisely to the details of care plans for my patients. I like behavior guidelines that ensure good and promised results.

There have been times when, in having to wait for God, that I wished I could curl up on the sofa with a volume of *Waiting for God for Dummies*, read it through in a single afghan-covered night on the couch, and emerge bleary-eyed but having a clear understanding of the right behavior for waiting for God. I have thought that if there were a Waiting 101 textbook, I could sit at my desk and memorize the language and the appropriate behavior for this new subject, waiting for God.

I discovered through this wait for the house to sell that all the guidance for God's waiting behavior was found in the book He authored, the Bible. One morning, God spoke distinctly to me through Paul's words in Titus 2:11–13. Paul wrote, "For the grace of God that brings salvation has appeared to all men. It teaches us to say no to ungodliness and worldly passions, and to live self-controlled, upright, and godly lives in this present age, while we wait for the blessed hope—the glorious appearing of our great God and Savior, Jesus Christ."

The first phrase, "For the grace of God," was a breath of fresh air that morning with the Lord. Brad and I love the word *grace*. To us it summarizes all that our Savior Jesus did for us at Calvary. It is the sum total of God's great love, mercy, forgiveness, and eternal life through Jesus Christ. It is the restoration of our souls to live fully in Him in this life and forever with Him in our eternal life. It is the promise of the Holy Spirit's moment-by-moment presence throughout the day, and the forgiveness for regretted momentary sins of any new day. That morning "For the grace of God" reminded me that my life had not only been saved in my Calvary experience with Jesus but that I gave my life to God to be guided through every day, be they moving forward, purposeful days or days of waiting for God's promise. We began to focus on the daily grace of God that was teaching us new lessons for this waiting-for-God time.

When our house did not sell, our real-estate agent suggested many options. Recarpeting was advised, as all potential buyers were now looking for homes with newly laid, neutral carpets. Driving by a recently sold home and seeing all the new Berber carpeting at the curb for trash pickup, we decided against that costly project. The possibility of a bridge loan was raised, citing it would secure the house we hoped to buy in South Carolina and give us needed extra time to sell the current house. In our spirits, we knew that God did not want us to burden ourselves financially that way.

Our now very frustrated agent suggested we bury a miniature statue of a saint in the front yard. The next day, I read in Psalm 20:7, "Some trust in chariots and some in horses, but we trust in the name of the Lord our God." We had already dismissed that front yard burial idea knowing this was not where the Lord would have us put our trust. We would say with the psalmist, our "trust is in the name of the Lord our God."

In our hearts we knew the time would eventually come to go on our great adventure with God. As the wait dragged on beyond

CHAPTER 4

advice on carpet, loans, and small statues, Brad remained calm and strong. He continually reminded me that it was a blessing to still be in our much-loved New Hampshire home. In spite of his reminders, my behavior began to look less like a trusting child of God and more like a weary pit survivor. Brad gently reminded me that we were blessed to be recipients of God's promise to lead us on a new adventure with Him in a new place and that we were witnesses of trusting God in this wait. Only half listening to his litany of encouragement, I asked God to show me what in the world self-controlled, upright, and godly living looked like while waiting.

The Patience Card

How many times when we are waiting for God do we have the patience card pulled out and waved in front of our faces? The same people who warn you not to pray for patience seem to have no reluctance about waving that card, and always seem to wave it in your weakest moments. The little breeze generated by the waving card brought tears to my eyes every time it was waved in my face. I wanted to snatch the card and tear it into bits. My mind was saying with ungodly impatience, "You have no idea how hard this is and how long I have been waiting." My pride was saying with downright impatience, "I have a promise from God. What do you know about that?"

God never fails to lead His children to a verse that will convict a prideful, impatient mind. Sometimes God even has to lead us back over familiar territory because we didn't learn all the lessons along the way. I didn't want to go back to some of those verses about waiting for God. I thought I had arrived at a firm place to stand. I reasoned that I was just missing a few behavioral guidelines! God led me back to Psalm 40:1–3, again. This time the opening phrase stopped me short on my supposedly firm place to stand. "I waited patiently for the Lord" revealed a behavior that pleases the Lord as He keeps us in the landscape of wait. Just as a writer aims to grab the reader's attention with strong opening sentences in each new chapter, so God will grab our attention in His opening words of each new chapter in the Bible when He has lessons to teach us.

Now it was God waving the patience card in front of me. This time the patience card's breeze refreshed me and caused me to understand that God had brought me out of the slimy pit and rescued me from despair to stand with Him right there on the rocky New Hampshire granite on a firm rock of trust. The psalmist continues in verse 3 with, "He put a new song in my mouth, a hymn of praise to our God." I cast around in my mind for my new song of praise. Immediately the melody and lyrics of the praise song, "In His Time," swept through my heart. The words reminded me that waiting is all about God's timing, not mine. The words reassured me God would not only do all that He told us, but would teach us His ways and make all the things He promised beautiful in His time.

The song became the theme song for our wait. My quiet-times began each morning with this song. It never failed to remind me that waiting for His promise was about learning His ways and trusting His timing. When doubts would come unbidden to my heart and mind, I would sing this song as a reminder that He would do just what He said He would do. And when another day ended with no sign of moving forward through our waiting time, I would sing this song as my evening prayer, this song of comfort and reminder that it would happen in His time. It was my desire that this song would always be a lovely, patient offering of praise to my Lord.

CHAPTER 4

The Psalms are rich with words to guide our times of waiting for God. The Psalms gave God's people in Old Testament days clear instructions for godly behavior for their long years of waiting for rescue from oppression and for the promised redemption of Israel, the coming of Messiah. The second behavior for waiting was revealed to me in Psalm 33:20, "We wait in hope for the Lord; He is our help and our shield." That behavior is hope. Paul ranks it very close to love, citing it as one of the three cornerstones of following Jesus as Lord: faith, hope, and love in 1 Corinthians 13.

The Lord not only is our hope as we wait, but He imbues us with His hope to help us and to shield us in the wait. This is not wishy-washy, "Gee, I hope so." Nor is it shoulder shrugging, "Golly gee, I hope the Lord will do what He said." This hope behavior that helps and shields is what is central to us when we have been rescued from despair and put on a firm place to stand. For us today, that is standing on the rock of Jesus Christ. This hope behavior is demonstrated throughout Scripture. It is seen in Noah as he sawed the lumber and pounded the nails that built the ark; and it is seen in Abraham as he walked up the mountain with his precious son Isaac, leading a donkey laden with firewood. This hope behavior is seen in Rahab as she grasped the scarlet cord out her Jericho wall window, and Esther as she stepped unbidden into the king's throne room. It is heard from Job as he proclaims to well-meaning friends, "Though He slay me, yet will I hope in Him," and from Paul and Silas in prison praying and singing songs of praise that helped their gospel witness and shielded them as the earthquake struck. Hopeful behavior joined our song of patient waiting and became central to our time of waiting for the Lord.

I said earlier that waiting *for* the Lord is not the same as waiting *on* the Lord. But waiting for God will not be done well without waiting on God through intimate times with Him. We cannot wait with patience and hope if we are not waiting at the feet of Jesus, waiting on the hope-filled presence of the Lord, and holding on to His promise for renewal. We can claim Isaiah 40:31 which says, "But those who hope in the Lord ["wait on the Lord" in KJV] will renew their strength. They will soar of wings like eagles; they will run and not grow weary, they will walk and not be faint." This is the renewed hope and strength the Lord wants to give us as we stand with Him, our rock and our salvation.

When God has spoken a word of promise and the wait for that promise lingers on with neither timetable nor guide, and when you find yourself suddenly in the darkened, unfamiliar landscape of wait and do not know what the Lord requires of you, listen for His song for waiting patiently. Put your eyes back on Jesus who is your hope, who will help and shield you as you put your hope in Him.

APPLICATION:

1. Evaluate your waiting behavior. What changes need to be made to wait with self-control, uprightness, and godliness?

2. Spend time with God. Thank Him for His patience with you.

3. Ask God for a theme song to ring out a melody of renewed trust in Him. Write out the song God has given you and sing it each morning to Him.

4. What renewed hope has God spoken to you today?

CHAPTER 5

A WOMAN FOR ALL SEASONS OF WAIT

*L*OOK ON THE *bright side! Every cloud has a silver lining! Don't worry! Be happy!* I have promised myself never to say this to those waiting or suffering. During our prolonged and often misunderstood wait, my unspoken response to these happy sayings from well-meaning friends is perhaps like your responses in your trial of wait. *Oh sure! Easy for you to say! You aren't walking in my shoes!* When the wait for God's promise to come lengthens, even as your hope is firmly placed in the One who has given you a promise, and even while you are singing praise songs of hope, happiness is often elusive.

James, whom I like to think of as James the practical, presents in his epistle to the Jewish believers a guide for Christian living. He opened his letter with a brief greeting and then this startling salvo, "Consider it pure joy, my brothers, whenever you face trials of many kinds, because you know that the testing of your faith develops perseverance" (James 1:2–3). The New King James Version has a bit of the pit mentality we spoke of in an earlier chapter, reading, "My brethren, count it all joy when you fall into various trials." *The Message* encourages us to see each trial as a "gift." The New Living Translation presents this as "an opportunity for joy." Whatever Bible translation or version you use, the message is plain: all followers of Jesus will face times of trials. In those trials, joy should partner with suffering and perseverance with developing maturity of faith. If our trial is one of waiting and our wait is one of suffering, how do we do this? How do we find the joy while we persevere? How in the world will we ever see our trial as a gift?

Abraham Lincoln is quoted as saying, "People are just as happy as they make up their minds to be." I was a failure at this kind of happiness. With teeth clenched and a smile pasted on my face, I made up my mind to happily navigate each day of waiting and present the attitude, "It is all in God's hands!" to all I met. Those who knew me well patted me on the shoulder, shaking their knowing heads. I had found hope but I relegated happiness to the promise, not to the wait.

Perhaps you are thinking that happiness and joy are really two different things. I agree. My experience showed me that when we fall off the joy wagon of faith into a pit of wait, the edges of the spiritual and natural blur in our minds. When tears fall from our eyes every time we go to God in prayer, our spiritual vision is so blurry we cannot see one reason for happiness. Soon our soul joy is depleted in the wait.

In the lives of women like Mary, everything, including happiness, was put on hold when breast cancer was found. Life was suddenly redefined by radiation, surgery, and chemotherapy. In Kim's life it was quickly depleted when her lone paycheck did not stop the pit of debt from growing nor ease the wait for new employment for her spouse. Happiness was deferred to the day the new job would be found and the debt load would be eased. For Elisabeth, joy was depleted when, after years of praying for her husband to come to faith in Christ, the promise God had given had not yet come to pass. She was soul weary and her joy well was empty in the wait for God's decades-old promise. True happiness was deferred to the day she would share the intimacy of faith in Christ with her husband.

Your wait, like my wait, is not a happy place to be. But James the practical tells us we are to count it all joy! Have you heard enough happy platitudes and Scriptures with a guilt zinger attached? Then let's examine a practical application of the way God refills our joy well. We need to see evidence for joy around us while we persevere in the landscape of wait.

Joy in the Seasons of Waiting

In James 5, he presents a pattern for waiting with joy and perseverance. In the context of waiting for the Lord's return, which so many of the early church thought would happen in their lifetime, we learn from the season-dependent life of a farmer. "Be patient, then, brothers, until the Lord's coming. See how the farmer waits for the land to yield its valuable crop and how patient he is for the autumn and spring rains. You too, be patient and stand firm, because the Lord's coming is near." Our journey through wait takes us down many roads. This road is a rural road of finding joy and perseverance in each season.

Brad and I lived for 30 years in a rural community in New Hampshire. We marked life there by the changes of the seasons and the farmers' work in the fields. The long winters when the fields are snow-covered give farm families time to plan gardens, order seeds, and repair tools. Spring's first sign, even before the last

CHAPTER 5

snowdrift melts under thick pine branches, is the placing of taps and the hanging of sap buckets on the centuries-old maple trees lining the winding road to our former home. Pussy willows begin to dot the stone wall edges of fields and robins return to build their nests. Spring breezes catch the sounds of tractors preparing the dormant fields, soon followed by the loamy smell of fresh-tilled, fertile soil. Acres of corn and fields of vegetables are planted, and the community hopes for necessary balance of sunshine and rain. Summer bursts with June heat onto the farm landscapes of New Hampshire. By July there is the sudden mushrooming of vegetable stands along every road, the farm children selling their gardens' bounty of corn, beans, and tomatoes. All too soon, the warmth of summer gives way to evening chill and the brilliant autumn oranges, reds, and yellows of those same sugar maple trees. The pumpkin fields and orchards fill with families collecting the last of the "yield of the farmer's valuable crop." Finally, coming full cycle is the first blanketing of winter white snows to protect and rest the fields.

James describes the farmer's crop as valuable. Valuable, too, are the lessons we reap as we look together at the seasons of waiting from a farmer's perspective, as we look at how trials and joy and perseverance and growth are found in each season.

Waiting and winter have more in common than the letter W. Both arrive as the bright colors of life leave our landscape. Both are bone chilling with the cold blasts of reality. Both have a beginning, but the end seems far off and completely out of our control. Like winter, the brightness of what was fades and the hope of what should be is buried by winter's cold white layers. The landscape is bleak, the sunshine is weak, and we are the lonely figure wandering through it. We say with King Richard III, "Now is the winter of our discontent."

But, "see how the farmer waits." He has learned he is not a farmer just when he is striding across the fields to sow seed, or walking through the growing stalks of corn, or picking the ripe garden produce for market. He knows he is a farmer every day of the long wait of winter for spring. We learn from this farmer that we must go through the waiting time to see hope spring up. Just as the farmer joyfully thinks about the new gardens, the new crops, and the new harvest as winter goes by, we can be joyfully thinking about one day experiencing God's promise when the healing comes, when the new job is offered, and when the beloved unbeliever is saved. And like the farmer who doesn't idly sit and dream longingly for spring but perseveres through the winter by ordering his seeds and preparing his tools, we can persevere by preparing our spiritual tools for the next season, deepening our prayer life, strengthening our knowledge of Scripture, and getting our hearts in order. When God brings to pass His promise, we will be ready!

Farmers watch for signs of spring. You may be watching for spring-like signs of hope from lab tests and CT scans. You may be waiting for a phone call and the hope-filled words, "Can you come in for a second interview?" You may be waiting for your beloved unbeliever to finally take a first small step toward faith, daring to darken the doors of your church.

Spring is the season of renewed promise. Spring is the season for seeds of hope. Abraham and Sarah had heard a threefold promise from God as they received the third of God's holy covenants. God promised to make them into a great nation, to bless them and all peoples because of them, and to protect them. When 24 years of waiting had passed and doubts spoke louder than hope, Abraham and Sarah experienced a *theophany*, a visitation from the Lord, who spoke renewed hope into their minds and relit the flame of promise in their hearts. You, too, may have waited through your own 24 long years, or even longer. Your comparably shorter 2-year wait may seem interminable and cruel. However long your time in the landscape of wait, listen with Sarah and Abraham to the promise of the Lord, "Is anything too hard for the Lord?" Let these holy words be the gentle spring rain that brings the first sustenance to the seed of hope God planted in your heart's soil. There is no disease God cannot heal. There is no job God cannot provide. There is no soul so stubborn God cannot save. If God has indeed spoken a word of promise and now trusts you to wait for His perfect timing, then these words from the Lord may be the first sign of spring. "Is anything too hard for the Lord?" (Genesis 18:14).

We think of summer as the perfect growing and ripening time for farm yields. We are eager to stop at the vegetable stands to bring home tender heads of lettuce; juicy, red tomatoes; sweet, silver and gold ears of corn; and fragrant, ripe melons. Are your taste buds working yet? As we enjoy our summer suppers, we don't think about the tilling, planting, fertilizing, pruning, and harvesting that the farmer did to produce this crop and get it to market for you and me. We have not concerned ourselves with how much sunshine was needed, how much rain was required, how much insect damage had occurred, and what profit could be earned. That has all been on the work- and worry-weary shoulders of the farmer. We simply enjoy this season of the farmer's life.

In the summer season of our wait, we find life is moving around us, even over us, oblivious to the frustrations of our too much pain, our too little rest, and our too many obstacles to seeing God's promise fulfilled. The weather may be a safe conversation starter in most circumstances, but not with the farmer who is watching his cash crop wither and die under a relentless sun. The daily news may be a good subject in most gatherings, but friends begin to avoid the question, *Anything new?* as they watch you wither in the face of your relentless trials and suffering. So where is the joy in the farmer's summer when the sun scorches the corn and the stalks turn brown long before harvest time? Is there a parallel for us in our wait?

I think the summer joy for this farmer in James is simply in being a farmer. In spite of the risks, his joy comes from his love of tilling the soil and growing the food that will feed people. The joy comes from a patient knowing that life does not depend on one season or even one year. He rests in the proven results of persevering. He accepts the fact that there will be bountiful times and lean times but that God will provide for all his needs as he waits through each season for the land to yield its valuable crop. He is not always happy with the trials of the changing seasons, but he always has a deep well of joy from which to draw.

Our joy in long summer waiting is knowing we are a child of the Most High God, created with gifts and talents to serve Him. Our joy is knowing the value of our life is not found in this present trial but is found in Christ Jesus. We are neither defined by our sufferings nor by our ability to persevere and find joy in the midst of them. Rather, we are defined by our relationship to the Author and Perfecter of our faith, Jesus. The farmer is not called a "droughter" in times of drought nor is he thought a washout when persistent heavy rains wash away his spring plants. He is a farmer for all seasons and all the trials that come his way. You, my friend, are not a waiter because you are waiting for God, nor are you a sufferer because of your trials God has allowed. You are a persevering child of the Most High God. You are a follower of Jesus who teaches us to "consider it pure joy" because He has chosen us and trusted us to walk with Him through the summer landscape of waiting for His precious promise.

New Hampshire's autumn leaves turning red, orange, and yellow called our family to a final visit at the local farm stand to pick the perfect pumpkins. The largest pumpkin would be carved by Brad and our daughter, Kim, into a happy face to welcome folks to our home. Midsize pumpkins would cluster with dried cornstalks and garlands of bittersweet at the lamp post. Smaller pumpkins would grace the center of our kitchen table. These were the final yield of the farmers' fields and labor, the final bustling days at the farm stands. The weary farm families smiled as pumpkins disappeared from their fields and the last of the vegetables were sold. They were ready for rest from their labor and enjoyment of reaping what they had sown.

Like the autumn colors of New Hampshire, the changing colors of the landscape of wait encourage our hearts. In the bleak trial of wait we are encouraged by the arrival of crisp, cool air and bright colors blanketing the landscape. We take a new look at our wait, see how far we have come on the journey, and discover a new energy for persevering in waiting. We look at our joy well and see that God has provided the exact needed amount of spiritual rain to fill our well with joy. We look into our heart and find it yielding valuable lessons that can only be learned in the landscape of wait.

In the autumn season of our wait, we discover that God created the seasons of our lives as well as the seasons of earth life. Each season is unique, purposeful, and critical to the harvest.

Just as one season follows another, so too must we experience the sequential seasons of wait. Autumn will come to an end, and so will the trial through which we wait.

The promise you have heard from God is as sure as the promise He gave His followers. All creation waits for the promised return of the Lord. In the meantime we can say with James the practical, "Be patient and stand firm, because the Lord's coming is near" (James 1:2).

APPLICATION:

1. How is your joy different from your happiness in life as you wait for God's promise?

2. Determine the current level of spiritual water in your joy well. How is your joy well being depleted? How is God replenishing it?

3. As you look at the landscape of your wait, what season do you see now? What are its identifying characteristics?

4. Describe the ways you have persevered in your own strength. What are the ways you will persevere in God's strength?

5. What lessons have you learned for waiting from James's farmer? How will you apply them to your waiting for God?

CHAPTER 6

E-WAITING

WE HAVE HEARD God's voice of promise, yet we have not seen His hand. We are waiting! "I wait for the Lord, my soul waits, and in His Word I put my hope. My soul waits for the Lord more than watchmen wait for the morning, more than watchmen wait for the morning" (Psalm 130:5–6). This verse is a wake-up call to waiting like the watchman for the dawn.

Waiting is not just an outward activity. Waiting is inward, deeply inward. Waiting is soul deep. As waiting becomes longer, the time of waiting for God's promise consumes us! It becomes our central focus, the lens through which life is now seen. For you it may be that hundreds of résumés have been sent and dozens of interviews have yet to produce the employment you are now desperate to have. Trust in God's promise to provide is strained as losing your home is imminent. Or, is it a prodigal child who has become increasingly entrenched in the drug scene, abandoning family and biblical values? The not knowing even where this child is leaves a dark hole in your heart into which God's promise to return her has disappeared. Like us, perhaps your house has not sold, and the downsizing to a retirement home and retirement living seems out of reach. This was not a life-threatening wait. Bankruptcy did not loom and drugs were not taking control of the life of one we loved. But waiting was consuming our life, for we had a promise. We had an adventure with God just out of reach.

When we first hear God's promise for new employment, for our child to return, or for our home to sell, we resolve to stand on that sure word from God. As time wears on, we may add, little by little, our own strength and our own resources to the wait, slowly watching our hope of soon experiencing God's promise dwindle. We cry out to God to restore our hope. We glue our eyes to every Scripture, knowing embedded in His Word are the words for hope's restoration. We fill up our minds with Scriptures that give strength to continue in hope. We think if we hope well today, the promise will come tomorrow. We think that real hope shortens our wait. Wrong on both counts. Hope is not defined by time.

Waiting While Hoping

Waiting and hoping are simultaneous activities when God chooses, trusts, and commands us to wait for Him. A night watchman knows about waiting. As the sky darkens, he watches the outlines of familiar shapes blur and blend into the night. No matter how dark the night, the night watchman knows dawn will come. He waits for the signs that dawn is near: the stars disappearing, blinking out one by one; the first streaks of pink and purple emerging in the blue black sky; the rooster crowing and birds awakening to sing a greeting to the new day. Of these signs the watchman is sure, and that his hope is sure, hope that morning surely approaches. What has been unseen in the dark will be revealed by the growing light. With the dawning of the new day, the landscape guarded is transformed from perilous to peaceful.

Night nurses also know about waiting for dawn. Early in my nursing career, I was a night nurse at the local hospital. Arriving long after the lights had been dimmed, we spoke with quiet voices and made rounds on our patients with pinpoints of light to monitor them and help them sleep. It was in the night that lonely patients whispered their greatest fears, often with dwindling hope for recovery. But as the sky began to lighten and the patient wakened to early morning nursing care, hope was renewed with the dawn of a new day and new possibilities. When hope dwindles, it is like the darkest time of night, the time just before dawn.

Like the night watchman, the night nurse, and the patients whose fears loom large in the night, we, too, can wait expectantly for the sure signs of God's impending dawn. These words from Psalm 130 are words of hope renewal. And, just as they wait eagerly for the signs of the dawning that ends the night watch, we can wait eagerly. Paul tells us in Romans 8:18–19, "I consider that our present sufferings are not worth comparing with the glory that will be revealed in us. The creation waits in eager expectation for the children of God to be revealed." Paul's words prove he understood e-waiting. Eager! Expectant!

Do *eager* and *expectant* describe you? Can you say with Paul, "I am eager and expectant no matter how long the night of wait"? Will you, after another year of waiting for God, still be eager and expectant? When the honeymoon stage of waiting is over, we quickly lose our grip on waiting. Our fingers loosen on our original hope. We discover we do not wait well for God.

CHAPTER 6

Creation gives us a measure of guidance from Romans 8:18–22 in *The Message*.

> *That's why I don't think there's any comparison between the present hard times and the coming good times. The created world itself can hardly wait for what's coming next. Everything in creation is being more or less held back. God reins it in until both creation and all the creatures are ready and can be released at the same moment into the glorious times ahead. Meanwhile, the joyful anticipation deepens.*

Creation waits eagerly and expectantly for God. Creation waits eagerly and joyfully because the Creator always gives more than we can ask or imagine, expectantly because He who created the world by speaking it into existence has spoken to us. God holds in His hands the promised answer and a perfect plan for us spiritually and physically in this life and in our eternal life.

Creation of this beautiful earth by God's own voice speaking it into existence occurred thousands of years ago, even millions of years ago, depending on what source you read and believe. Our lifetime is but a speck on the continuum of time, from creation to the Lord's return. Even so, in our short lifespans we are witnesses of God's creation. We climb the tallest mountains He formed to see our panoramic countryside. We look over the edge and down deep into the wondrous Grand Canyon He carved. We sail far out on the deep blue waters He called to be and know we will eventually see land on the distant shore. We see the galaxies through a telescope and the miniscule microbes through a microscope. What have you in your lifespan seen that proclaims the creation and the Creator? That is the creation that can hardly wait for what will be in that glorious time ahead when Christ returns.

Without eagerness in waiting to see His plan unfold, and without the expectation of God suddenly acting on our behalf, our focus stays on our suffering in the wait. Like creation, we can have deep, soul-felt, joyful anticipation when we allow the Spirit to revitalize our hope for God to move as He has promised when all is ready. We must say with Paul, "Our present sufferings are not worth comparing with the glory that will be revealed in us." You may be out of work, but you do not need to be out of hope. You may have lost a child to the clutches of the world, but God has His hand outstretched to him. You may have a home that has not sold, but you can watch for it eagerly and expect it to happen with the dawn of a new day.

It is time for e-waiting, being on our tiptoes to see the first dawning glimpse of His work, having every spiritual nerve ending attuned to the almighty powerful God for whom we wait. Be more watchful than the night watchman. For morning is coming, as we wait with eagerness and expectancy the joyful anticipation of Scripture's fulfillment.

CHAPTER 6

APPLICATION:

1. What has been the darkest hour of your waiting time?

2. List ways creation reminds you to wait for God's promise.

3. What are some ways you can wait expectantly in the dark?

4. How do others see in you signs of eagerness for God's coming promise even as you wait?

CHAPTER 7

AN EXPECTANT HEART FOR WAITING

"WELL WORTH WAITING for!" is a hindsight exclamation of joy! Those who have experienced a particular situation of wait tell us what we are waiting for will be well worth the wait! No argument there. I have not regretted waiting for God's answers to prayers and promises to be fulfilled, or waiting for His plans for our life to unfold. Waiting expectantly for our unplanned child to be born, He spoke provision to my worried heart. Waiting hopefully for my husband to step into life with Christ, I heard God speak assurances to my hurting heart. Waiting impatiently for our home to sell, I experienced God's unleashed lessons for my doubting heart. Waiting with frustration for opportunities to do medical missions, God's voice said, "In My time and in My way!"

Waiting Shows Us God's Plan

Kimberly tells me that all she ever wanted out of life, nothing more and nothing less, was to marry and be a mother. When her childhood friends voiced ambitious dreams of becoming

CHAPTER 7

astronauts, doctors, and nurses, Kimberly's dream was to become a wife and mother. With so many career fields now wide open for women, we don't often hear such family-centric goals voiced. Going against the trends of her peers, Kimberly created a simple three-step plan for her life: marry a Christian man who would cherish her, buy a home to prepare for their future family, and then have two or maybe four children to complete this perfect plan. Her life would be committed to loving and caring for her family in their home. Her joy would be complete when her dreams and plans became reality. Marrying her high school sweetheart, Mel, soon after graduation, the young couple attended college together and worked diligently to buy a first home. Just before their college graduation they signed papers for their first home, completing step two in Kimberly's life plan. Celebrating the blessings of life, they pursued the plan's third step—a child!

One month became two months. Many more months passed, wearing on into years. Kimberly and Mel's landscape of wait was bleak, peopled by doctors and nurses and technicians garbed in white lab coats and blue scrubs. Painful monthly injections and daily medicine that turned her sweetness into grumpiness preceded complicated procedures to fulfill Kimberly's now not-so-simple plan for her life.

She says, "I can truly say I have never been more miserable in my life." Looking back on those nine long years, Kimberly identifies naïveté about the reality of many couples' struggles to bear children. She also names anger as her greatest emotion, a fist-raising anger at God causing her to ask over and over, "How could You do this to me?" Kimberly's prayertime filled with questions you, too, may have asked God from the depths of your own barrenness: *Why did You instill in me such a love for children if*

You were going to do this to me? What kind of a loving God are You who would allow 14-year-old girls to have babies when You won't allow me to do the same? Why would You punish me like this when I ask for so very little from You?

As anger filled the barren places of Kimberly's heart and mind, praying ceased and her heart hardened to the things of God. Reluctantly she attended church at Mel's insistence, her tears marking the pages of her Bible as she heard preached again and again of how loving and faithful God is to His people. Anger took a 180-degree turn, from Kimberly directing her anger at God to her imagining God's anger directed at her. The idea that God had judged her and found her too wanting as a wife and as a Christian to bear a child crashed into her mind. Her anger turned upon herself as she began to believe her barrenness was punishment from God.

In the midst of Kimberly's dark confusion, while working at her computer, she searched through adoption sites on the Internet. Adoption had crossed Kimberly's and Mel's minds, but the desire for their own biological child impeded them from pursuing that means to become parents. Quickly Kimberly found a Web site and the picture of a little boy named Nikolay in the Ukraine appeared. His olive skin, dark eyes, and dark hair were much like Mel's. As she and her husband looked at Nikolay, her heart began to yearn for this child. Both began to pray for God's guidance, Mel eager to begin the adoption process but Kimberly struggling with substituting adoption for a biological child. Weeks later, God's peace began to seep into her heart to lead her to create their family through adoption.

They began the long process of adopting Nikolay. With each step an inexplicable uneasiness grew in Kimberly's heart as she prayed. With a heavy heart she cried out to God, "Lord, tell me what You are trying to tell me. Help me see Your will." Through her tears, she blindly reached for the nearby book of daily devotions. The devotional for that day centered on the rewards of waiting. The Scripture, Psalm 27:13–14 (NKJV), "Wait on the Lord; be of good courage, and He shall strengthen your heart; wait, I say, on the Lord!", spoke volumes to her waiting heart. The devotional writer compared waiting to carefully baking a cake. Taking it from the oven halfway through the necessary baking time would make it unfit for eating. Just as we should not want a half-baked cake, we should not rush God's timing for His promises and settle for a half-baked promise.

Kimberly related to the example given of Hannah waiting "year by year" to conceive and bear a child. She knew all too well the disappointment of living month to month and year to year like Hannah. Writing in her journal she concluded with, "God knows what you need. Don't give up and try to satisfy that need your own way. Wait on Him, and He will take care of you according to His goodness." Yet, confusion overwhelmed Kimberly as she angrily cried out to God, "Why are You playing with my emotions? God, I know You were telling me to adopt. Why are You now telling me not to adopt? I don't understand!"

Days passed as Kimberly's emotions reeled from one extreme to another. Like Hannah, taking her frustrations and hopes to her God brought surrender and trust in the wait. Finally, Kimberly prayed, writing these words in her journal: "Father, I know You are in control of my life and I want nothing more than for You to lead me on Your path. I surrender it all to You. My life, my dreams, my passions—they are all Yours." With that moment of surrender, she felt peace for the first time in more than three years. A new Hannah-like patience filled the next few months as Kimberly and Mel terminated adoption proceedings for Nikolay and waited for God to reveal His plan. She now had a promise from God, and this time she would wait His way and for His time.

Just when patience and trust hallmarked her landscape of wait, God allowed another hindrance to derail her. Kimberly's family had been uneasy about the possibility of adoption. When the news that Kimberly's sister, married just two months, was quickly pregnant, all the pain of the past years' wait surged into her heart. With it came the fear that if they did adopt, their child would be loved less than her sister's child. Seeing this new, deep pain overcome their daughter, her parents urged them now to adopt. But because of this new fear of a less-loved child, she steeled her heart not to pursue the adoption process, even though that decision would leave them childless.

God interrupted her secret resolve never to adopt with a phone call from her dad. He was weeping over the death of a pet rabbit Kimberly had purchased for eight dollars, 14 years ago. He called her, not just to break the sad news, but to say he now understood the deep love adoption of a child would bring into their lives. He told her, "Surely, if he loved the adopted pet rabbit and shed tears over its death, how much more their family would love a child brought into their life to grandparent through adoption." Kimberly's final fear was erased in that moment. That call from her dad was the green light of go from God.

Kimberly and Mel pursued adoption and the process was seamless, not a single bump in their new road. Arriving in Russia at the orphanage with which their adoption agency had connected them, they met Alexander and Angelina, twins who would soon be their children. Blonde and blue-eyed like Kimberly, these two tiny orphans, who were not available for adoption until the very day of their new parents' arrival, were the reason for their waiting. They were the reason God gave them their wait and then their family. Kimberly writes, "We brought them into our family, and although it wasn't the way I had planned it, I was finally a mother and it was the best feeling in the world!"

As Kimberly looks back on her wait, she knows God was not punishing her with the wait, but was blessing her. She believes God chose her and Mel to be adoptive parents by instilling them with a love so strong for children and a desire so strong to be parents that they would travel thousands of miles to fulfill God's plan for their lives. Now when people ask her about their children, it is her opportunity to share God's love with them. Kimberly explains that these children were sent straight from God. Their part was to wait for God to lead them through their personal "fullness of time," perfect God plan, to Russia.

While in Russia, the adoption agency spoke of another child, Alexander and Angelina's three-year-old sister. She was in an orphanage 200 miles away and not available for adoption. No further explanation was given nor information available. Returning home with their beautiful new children, the unseen face of a three-year-old sister persistently called to their hearts in quiet moments. Kimberly wrote adoption agencies in Russia hoping to hear of the sister's release for adoption. She visited Web sites for adoptive parents to see if she recognized anyone writing about the child's adoption. For nearly two years they prayed diligently for her to be given a loving home somewhere and somehow. They could not bear the idea that the sister to the children God had given them, that they loved with all their hearts, might be doomed to orphanage life and life without hearing about Jesus. Silence greeted all their inquiries.

That silence was the calm before the rush of God into their lives with a phone call from Russia. The sister was available. Could they come to Russia now?! Mel and Kimberly's life lit up with a new joy and turned upside down with quick preparations to go. They felt compelled to return to Russia, for this child, in their hearts, already was theirs; this child who would finish the baking of the cake in Kimberly's long-ago devotional reading. They felt great peace that this was God's fullness of time for them.

With the trip to Russia hurriedly being planned came a revelation. "I no longer yearned to have a child. We were having the children meant for us." She could now see in Angelina and Alexander their own family traits and mannerisms other parents saw in their children. She could even see her own daddy's eyes in one of the twins. Mel and Kimberly returned from Russia on a cool November day with big sister Carley, completing their family almost two years to the day after arriving home with the twins. They had much for which to thank God as they celebrated Thanksgiving. The words of Ephesians 3:20 filled their hearts and they praised God saying: "Now to him who is able to do immeasurably more than all we ask or imagine, according to his power that is at work within us."

If you are thinking Carley was the immeasurably more of their heart, you are correct. But God had even more to give them, more than they could ask or imagine. Three months later, as Kimberly and Mel basked in the contentment of family life with their three blessings from God, came the news Kimberly was pregnant. Kimberly tells me with a laughing voice, "I think God was saying, 'Kimberly, you harassed Me for so long, I am giving

CHAPTER 7

you one more.'" Kaitlin was born one year after Carley came into their family. With four children in three years, their hearts, like their home, were full to overflowing with the shouts and laughter of children's voices.

Many who find they are waiting for God discover the same truths Kimberly found. Although your wait may not revolve around having children or building a family, Psalm 27:14 (NKJV), "Wait on the Lord; be of good courage, and He shall strengthen your heart," resonates with each of our waiting hearts. It is in the midst of waiting for God's promise that our hearts are made strong to wait. It is only His strength that enables us to navigate through the landscape of wait. As we emerge from waiting, we discover then the "immeasurably more" of God. And sometimes we are blessed with God's "more than we can ever ask for or imagine."

APPLICATION:

1. How has anger appeared in your wait for God? Where have you directed the anger?

2. Describe a new direction from God that is different than the hopes and dreams that caused you to wait.

3. When you have been on track with God in waiting, what events have caused you to derail?

4. How has God provided strength to your heart to wait?

5. If your wait is behind you, what is your "immeasurably more," your "more than you could ever ask or imagine" from God?

CHAPTER 8

HOLY SPIRIT POWER FOR WAITING

*I*N MATTHEW 28:20 Jesus promised He would be with us to the end of the ages. This holy promise leaves out no road or landscape, even when the journey to God's promise seems to take years and seems to be taking us to the emotional ends of the earth. We may feel alone in the landscape of wait and find ourselves isolated from those who have forgotten we have a promise. All around us seem to be living\ in the present-day blessings of God, their promises fulfilled by beautiful babies, saved spouses, and once-rebellious children now restored. When our life feels bereft of any blessings, where do we find the power to push on in our wait for another month, another year, or for a lifetime? Turn to Luke 2. There we have a glimpse into the lives of a two empowered figured waiting to see God's promise fulfilled.

First there is Simeon, whose name, according to biblical name scholars, means to hear, obey, and understand. Hebrew children's names in biblical times were never about popularity but about meaning. This could represent the situation around

CHAPTER 8

their conception—as with *Isaac*, which refers to Sarah's laughter (Genesis 21:6); or with events of birth as we see with Esau's and Jacob's names referring to their appearance at birth—*hairy* and *heel holding* (Genesis 25:25–26).

As life continued, the Hebrews began to name their children for the qualities they hoped would be seen in them, infinitely better choices than hairy and heel holding. Simeon's parents were visionary with their name choice for their son *Simeon: one who hears, obeys, and understands.*

Simeon heard a promise from God! Read Luke 2:25–35 to capture a glimpse of the Holy Spirit empowerment presented there. Luke, writing with the accurate details demanded by physicians then and now in assessing critical situations, gives us three critical spirit "power points" for waiting.

Simeon first shows us the Holy Spirit power comes to those who are actively listening in their wait. We can infer Simeon is in his final earth years from Luke's record of Simeon's words, "You now dismiss your servant in peace." Various Scripture translations are consistent in their description of Simeon as righteous and just and devout. And as we look at our Bibles, we see that Simeon is e-waiting for the promise he heard from God, given to us in verse 26, "that he would not die before he had seen the Lord's Christ." Simeon is further reported to have been "eagerly waiting for the Messiah to come" in the New Living Translation. In *The Message*, he is described as "a man who lived in the prayerful expectancy of help for Israel." Eager and expectant! There had not been a prophet for 400 years, but Simeon believed in the Holy Spirit–revealed promise that his own eyes would see Messiah before he died. There had been no new prophetic words from God's people, no fresh voice declaring the soon coming of Messiah, but Simeon heard the promise of God spoken by the Holy Spirit.

Simeon had eager ears! The Holy Spirit empowers us through prayer to have eager ears to hear God's promise and an expectant heart to believe that what our ears have heard, our eyes will see.

It was in the basement laundry room of our first little ranch house that God spoke to my spirit's eager ears. I was staining the new shelves Brad had installed for me. While kneeling, carefully sweeping the brush back and forth across the new wood, I began to pray for Brad's salvation. Over the past year, it had become increasingly clear that my beloved but unbelieving husband would not quickly begin attending church with me nor pay attention to Christ. I was responsible for this landscape of wait. I had willingly walked into married life with the man of my dreams, but not of God's plan, not yet. My ears had been eager only to hear the words Brad and I shared of growing love and future marriage. No one opposed our plans, the normal plans of two deeply in love young adults, both raised in a Baptist church. All presumed we would settle down in married life and return to living a Christian lifestyle. I was on track, but on the spiritual journey alone.

My laundry room prayer began with a long list of reasons God should not delay, but call Brad back to faith now. They were somewhat self-centered reasons for our family, but driven by love for my husband and concern for his eternal destination. God seemingly listened to each reason patiently. When I paused for breath with the last sweep of the brush, God spoke to my eager ears with these words, "I love Brad more than you, more than you can ever love him. Brad is Mine to save!" Those words of Holy Spirit promise seemed to bounce audibly off the paneled walls of that basement laundry room. Those words of Holy Spirit promise were the beginning point of Simeon-like prayerful expectancy!

CHAPTER 8

Full of this new prayer expectancy, I joined a group of five women at our little Southern Baptist church in New Hampshire. We met each week to pray for the needs of our family. Brad's salvation figured among the prayer needs shared; needs for ministry, employment, and children. Brad's commute home coincided exactly with this weekly prayertime. One night he greeted me with the story of hearing someone calling his name while driving. He heard his name called again, and then called again to the point where he pulled off the highway to check the car trunk. As he told me this, my eager ears heard again the Holy Spirit promise. I knew whose voice was calling Brad's name, calling him to salvation. At that very time, the five women had been praying expectantly to the One who loved him so deeply.

Second, Simeon shows us the Holy Spirit power will move us to obey Him as we wait for the promise. God enrolled me in the Holy Spirit School for Waiting. God gave me 1 Peter 3 as my textbook. There I found the lessons to be learned and the commands to be obeyed. If you think I am pulling out the "be submissive to your husbands" Bible verse report card, you are wrong. It was the subject of verse 4 that God led me to major in: "the unfading beauty of a gentle and quiet spirit." God was calling me to rely on His empowering to learn to be gentle and have a quiet spirit as I waited for the promise of Brad's salvation.

I did not get all A's in the Holy Spirit School for Waiting. There were many days when my homework was barely passing, not because the Holy Spirit power was absent, but I because I had not accessed that resource. But God is able to keep His promises in spite of those who wait for it. I keep in my Bible the testimony Brad wrote for me to read at his baptism. Dr. Jim Wideman, our pastor, asked each person being baptized to prepare a brief testimony of faith to be read just before being immersed. Brad wrote several words of his faith in Jesus as Lord and Savior and closed with these words, "I want to thank all of you who have prayed for me to take this step—especially my wife, Debby. Her unwavering love for the Lord and the peace that she received from Jesus set an example that could not be denied." Yes, that last phrase was read with an emotionally unsteady voice. I realized that Brad was speaking of the grace God had given me to wait for His promise with a gentle and quiet spirit . . . the peace from Jesus that my husband recognized in my landscape of wait.

And third, Simeon shows us the Holy Spirit will give us understanding when the promise is fulfilled. Brother Jim, as he was called in our church, was a great encourager to me as I waited, and to Brad as he came to faith. Brother Jim asked me to consider leading a session during Discipleship Training on Sunday evenings for women also waiting for their husbands' salvation. I agreed to do this even though I was still in that landscape of wait for the promise of God, even though I thought there were still lessons to be learned and challenges to overcome. The morning our church spiritually rocked with Brad's near run up to the altar to profess his faith in Jesus publicly, followed by clapping and happy tears by our church family, Brother Jim said it was not a coincidence that the Beloved Unbeliever Class would begin that night. The Holy Spirit helped me understand God was about to unleash His Holy Spirit power in the lives of women praying for their husband's salvation. The women needed to see God's promise of salvation to all who believe fulfilled, demonstrated in our life.

CHAPTER 8

A Song Still Being Sung,
A Painting Still Being Finished

Simeon burst into a God song of praise as he held the infant Messiah. These words of high and holy praise from Simeon's promise-fulfilled heart have been sung for centuries by Christians. The *Nunc Dimittis,* as his praise song is referred to in liturgical music, is traditionally sung, or even chanted, as an evening prayer. It is found in the 1662 Anglican Book of Common Prayer and is part of both the Roman Catholic and Lutheran service of Compline. Charles Spurgeon titled a sermon from this passage "Simeon's Swan Song," indicating it is Simeon's farewell of praise to His promise-keeping God and announcement to the world that has waited for God's salvation, "a light for revelation to the Gentiles and for glory to your people Israel."

Not only Simeon's Spirit-inspired song has endured, but his Holy Spirit–led understanding has stood the test of *anno Domini* years of time. Simeon spoke prophetic truth to Mary and Joseph and all who witnessed this confirmation of the infant Messiah in the Temple.

There is never too much praise or proclamation about Jesus. As if this were an unfinished painting of Mary and Joseph standing in awe as old Simeon held Jesus, sang a song of praise, and then prophesied the future of their child, the new parents moved through Jerusalem's temple courts to encounter elderly Anna to complete the picture of God's promise fulfilled. Anna, a woman widowed after only seven years of marriage, had lived the remainder of her life in fasting and praying, never leaving the temple, but living a worshipful life in the Temple as she waited for Messiah. Proficient in patient waiting and in prophesying, when

Anna encountered Baby Jesus, she immediately gave thanks to God; and new prophecy spilled from her heart as she spoke of the child to all who shared her Messiah wait and the redemption of Jerusalem.

Mary and Joseph took Baby Jesus to Jerusalem thinking they were presenting their child to the Lord, according to Mosaic law. God's plan to fulfill His promise of Messiah turned this around, presenting the baby Lord Jesus to Simeon and Anna, who were living devout and prayerful lives, and confirming the lordship of this child. The young couple bridged the days of Old Law and Old Covenant living by the elderly faithful who waited for Messiah, with the birth of Jesus who would fulfill the Law and bring the New Covenant of salvation to all who would believe.

Israel's landscape-of-wait painting stood unfinished for hundreds of years. Is your landscape of wait painting unfinished? Has it stood untouched too long? Is there someone you love deeply, central to all your hopes and dreams and prayers, who has not yet fallen in love with the Savior? Do you, though married, walk spiritually alone? Are you a child of God, but the parents you love have not yet come into the family of God? Is your dearest sibling or closest friend still resistant to the gospel love of Jesus? It can be a long wait for our landscape picture to be completed with the one we love and pray for coming to saving faith. But we can learn from Simeon and Anna that when God speaks a promise, it will be fulfilled. When our ears have become eager ears and our praying life expectant, we will be able to walk steadily through the landscape of wait with the Lord who is Promise personified.

APPLICATION:

1. Write again the promise you heard from God.

2. What are the three Holy Spirit power points we learn from Simeon?

3. In what ways are you listening to God with eager ears?

4. Prayerful expectancy described Simeon. Rate your prayer expectancy level from 1 to 5, with 5 being highest.

   _____ Praising God, certain His promise will come in His perfect timing.

   _____ Praising God, hoping you will see His promise fulfilled.

_____ Praying for God to speed up His timeline.

_____ Pleading with God for your promise to come now and end the wait.

_____ Doubting God will do what He said if He even spoke at all.

5. Describe the lessons you are learning in the Holy Spirit School for Waiting.

6. Understanding will come when God's promise is fulfilled and the landscape painting completed. Who is the yet-to-be-painted figure in your landscape of wait?

CHAPTER 9

OUR WAIT IS NOT YOUR WAIT

FAMILY PRACTICE MEDICINE was the focus of my nursing career. The waiting room in our office had dozens of chairs which were filled and refilled throughout the day by patients coming and going, waiting for appointments or tests. Conversations among those waiting drifted back to the nurses' area whenever the door opened and the next patient was called in. "What are you seeing the doctor for?" began many a waiting room conversation. Although strangers, waiting room patients seemed comfortable asking that question or relating their own medical problems with other waiting patients. Symptoms, diseases, and treatments were described in great detail as if it were grand rounds in a teaching hospital. I also heard well-meaning but thoughtless statements. "Oh, I had that! It's nothing compared to my problem." "I'm sorry to hear that. My uncle died from it in a week, but I'm sure you'll be fine." Words meant as encouragement or sympathy from well-meaning people dot the landscape of wait.

In family practice nursing, my doctor and I could see upward of 40 or more scheduled patients a day. We cared for a wide range

CHAPTER 9

of patient needs, from common colds to rare metabolic diseases; from ongoing chronic illness to emergency medical situations. Routine health care was provided for every generation of our families, from tiny newborns carried to us in baby seats to the very elderly brought for their appointments in wheelchairs. No two patients arrived in our waiting room with the same need or left with the same treatment. Each waited, but each wait was different.

Some have appropriately described the place where we wait for God as His waiting room because of the suffering experienced there and the desperate hope placed in the Great Physician there. Sermons have been preached and books have been written using this waiting room metaphor. Perhaps my familiarity with waiting rooms, not only as a nurse but as one who has waited there, has given me another description. Waiting with other soon-to-be grandparents for a new baby, waiting as a praying wife with my husband having surgery, and waiting as the reassuring oldest of Mother's children when she had open-heart surgery, I discovered waiting rooms are a short-term place for waiting. The prolonged wait is more like a bleak landscape one must continue to live in and move through until God's promise is fulfilled. We had spent a brief time in God's waiting room, but had been moved out to this new place and new way to wait.

Navigating through the landscape of wait for our home to sell, we met others who had experienced a similar wait to sell their homes. We heard, "Oh, we went through that. It's nothing compared to what we are going through now after losing our jobs when the shipyard downsized. We cannot find work in this economy." True! We were not waiting for employment after losing a job, we were retiring early according to God's instructions to us. We were not in a financial crisis, yet. Brad had already retired and my retirement date loomed on the horizon. My position as nurse manager in our bustling five-physician family practice office would soon be reduced to being one of several per diem nurses. But only partly true, because we had heard the promise of God for a new adventure; heard the direction of God to retire, sell our home, and journey with Him to a new place to live and serve.

Words from well-meaning people were often heard drifting across the landscape of our wait. "Your house hasn't sold yet? I'm sorry to hear that, but I'm sure you'll be fine." "It's a seller's market. Ours sold in a week." I did not feel fine with their words meant to encourage me or feel fine about our prolonged wait. I did not want to hear how quickly other homes sold. Theirs had been a waiting room experience. We were now in a broad, no-end-in-sight landscape. Their stories sounded similar, but it wasn't the same as our story. Their words, meant to encourage us, served only to set me back in our wait and caused me to want to shout . . . *Our wait is not your wait!*

Each Wait Is Unique

Scripture speaks to the uniqueness of our waits. We do well to read the Book of Exodus to observe the wisdom of Moses who learned from a burning bush experience how to both *go for* the Lord and to *wait for* the Lord. He obediently went back to Egypt, went back to the Pharaoh, and went back to the enslaved Hebrew people. He waited for Pharaoh's mind to be changed by God, waited for the promised plagues and protection, and waited for the exact time of the promised exodus of God's people to be fulfilled.

The books of Law, the Pentateuch, the first five books of the Old Testament, were written by Moses. Each book entwines

CHAPTER 9

humankind's early history, particularly Hebrew nation history, with the law and purposes of God for man, even twenty-first-century man. God entrusted Moses with writing His law because it was Moses who heard God's voice speak it, because Moses consulted with God in all things and for every decision, and because Moses obeyed God's law.

An incident in the early history and writing of the law occurs in Numbers 9 and demonstrates Moses' reliance on God for counsel in all things. On the one-year anniversary of the exodus from Egypt, God instructed Moses to call the people to celebrate Passover, the night of God's passing through Egypt when He struck down all who were the firstborn of man and of livestock. God passed over the doors of His people with the blood of the lambs on the doorframes. This memorial celebration was to be held "in accordance with all its rules and regulations" outlined the night of that first Passover.

Because of a death and subsequent contact with the deceased, some were ceremonially unclean and could not celebrate Passover. Imagine yourself in this situation, wanting to celebrate the greatest event yet in Israel's history, the Exodus, but a death in the family prevents it. These men, on that same day of Moses' celebration announcement, went to Moses with their disappointment and their question, "Why should we be kept from presenting the Lord's offering with the other Israelites at the appointed time?" (Numbers 9:7).

Moses immediately sees the uniqueness of their situation, answering them with, "Wait here until I have received instructions for you from the Lord" (Numbers 9:8 NLT). This wait-for-God Scripture reminds us that in our humanity, even the wisest among us may not have the answer. It reminds us that we can bring our questions of what seems so unfair in life to the Lord. It is great assurance to know God is the source of answers and instructions for our wait. In Numbers we see God was ready to give special instructions for their unique situation. God made provision for them and held them accountable to His instructions. It was great assurance to these men, as it should be for us, to know God does not hold us accountable for circumstances beyond our control; instead He makes a way for us to live in obedience to Him.

An Example of the Waiting Father

As we have explored God's instructions for waiting for His promise through the words of David, Jeremiah, Luke, and Simeon, Jesus gives us a parable that addresses a particular purpose of waiting and demonstrates how to wait as Father God waits. In the landscape of waiting for the return of a prodigal child or family member, there is wide variation of circumstances. What lures our children out of homes and churches, out of following Jesus' lifestyle, varies greatly.

In a world of many voices, the voice of God calling our children to live devotedly to Him may be drowned out by the cacophony of worldview noise, drowned out by the shouting voice of world pleasure saying, *Hey! Don't listen to your Father calling you! Come have fun with me!* Or it may be drowned out by the voice of prestige and riches shouting, *You can have it all! You deserve it all! Follow me, not Him!* Our hearts break as we watch our children heed the call of the world and follow a road that leads to the dark world of pain and suffering disguised as freedom and fun living, or follow a yellow brick road of worldview success to an emerald city that holds only superficial hope and false promise.

CHAPTER 9

Jesus gives us the parable of the prodigal son as an example through the waiting father of how to live in the landscape of wait for the return of our own prodigal child—son or daughter, sister or brother, grandson or granddaughter. Jesus shares from His incarnate heart and the heart of His faithful Father God ways to live while we wait for their return from following one of these world voices down roads of spiritual and physical destruction. Luke 15:11–24 gives us the portion of this famous parable we will consider here. Read through it and put yourself in the waiting sandals of the earthly father. Watch for the unique characteristics of his wait for the beloved child to return.

Many of us in reading this parable say we would not be like this earthly parent, giving our children everything they ask for, certainly not their inheritance now when they are young and irresponsible. Maybe not. But I know parents who have depleted their investments or retirement to provide treatment programs and counseling for their addicted children, providing it not just once but over and over. I know well-meaning parents who have cheered their children on in their pursuit of wealth, contributing to the acquiring of possessions that represent the lifestyle of success long before they have attained it on their own. Others without the financial ability are masters of *enabling*, that apt term for personal investment in keeping their addict or alcoholic prodigal child safe, preventing him from taking responsibility for his actions and the consequences and always making excuses for him to friends, family, and God.

Are you thinking if you saw your child heading down one of these roads, you would do whatever it takes to stop her? Some of you would. Many parents of prodigals have done all they could to keep their children walking with Jesus. Some have ignored behavioral signs until the situation is out of control. When we have not parented a prodigal child, we think there must be some early warning system and a way to constrain the child. We believe God will give us a way to intercept and redirect her. Sometimes there is and our interceptions will redirect them. But because choice is part of our God-created DNA, we cannot force our children to choose to follow Jesus.

In Jesus' parable, when we see the father as Father God, who when His child spiritually says, "Let me choose my own way," He does not constrain him, force him to deny himself, and take up his cross and follow Jesus. This heavenly Father's plan is for all His children to faithfully stay in kingdom life. When they choose to go, this Father God knows the road they take. He knows every twist and turn and pothole. He knows the squandering of resources and life they will experience. He knows the lessons they need to learn through pain and suffering. We read this parable and say we would never let our child end up in squalor with only a slop bucket in hand. This Father God says the lessons are not found in high living like this prodigal, with wild living, but are found in the lowest places of life, like our prodigal here in the pigsty.

Waiting while your child is squandering his or her life can be a tug-of-war between going and rescuing to save what is left, to staying and waiting to see if all the good parenting and spiritual guidance you have given will kick in and your child will come home. Emotions vacillate in your heart; one moment in rage at your child's stupidity, the next in despair at the waste of a promising Christian life. Prayers move from asking God to protect and restore the child to begging God to not let him or her die. For some with long landscapes of waiting for a prodigal, a day arrives

CHAPTER 9

when all the words of love and worry, parental pain and anguish are erased with the single tap of the delete key, leaving the child in a place of apathy and hopelessness. No two people with love for a prodigal have the same waiting story. We all love the fact that while feeding the pigs the prodigal finally came to his senses. Back up a phrase and take note. This is crucial. "No one gave him anything." This is part of the model of waiting Jesus presents. When prodigal children are in post-squandering mode, no one is to give them anything. Their new friends have abandoned them when the money ran out and when the success became failure. Their former friends have lost their trust in them. Their families have been hurt too many times to take them in or give them a handout. Prodigals do not come to their senses unless they are left with only their thoughts and the whispers of the Holy Spirit. Reminders of home and goodness and fulfillment will only fill their heads and hearts with longing when you wait for them to reach their "bottom," their lowest point, their hopeless point, their most empty point in life. This is the hardest waiting, the "what if they die in the pigsty?" waiting.

From a human perspective, how was the prodigal's father able to wait, knowing his son had chosen to live in a far country and in a world-inspired lifestyle that threatened his life and soul? Did the squandering of his own released riches reach his ears through the Israelite grapevine? Did rumors of wild living flash before his eyes like our scrolling through revealing Facebook pictures? Be assured, God hears your heartbroken prayers pleading with Him to protect and save them. Be assured, God will give you staying power to wait for their return. Be assured, God's Holy Spirit will speak to them, calling to them to return to their senses. The choice remains theirs.

Scripture tells us this father waited vigilantly. Luke 15:20 (NLT) tells us, "So he returned home to his father. And while he was still a long way off, his father saw him coming. Filled with love and compassion, he ran to his son, embraced him, and kissed him." Apparently much time has passed, for much wealth was squandered. But life has gone on at home. The older brother and the father are working the land together. There are servants in the house and fat calves in the pasture. Wait has not consumed this father; neither has it been set aside. Like this father, we have other children, or other grandchildren and siblings. They are making good decisions and living faithful, Christ-centered lives. Our wait must not keep us at the door watching. We must be fully invested in their lives while hoping for the prodigal's return.

Every day, many times a day, the father looked down the road hoping to see the beloved child walking toward home. Does your heart leap when the phone rings and you hope it is your daughter, your son, your sister? Does your mind imagine the many scenarios of what the day might be like when you look out and there she or he is? Do you write and rewrite in your mind what the best words will be to say when your beloved child returns? Here we learn we will not need a written script for our reunion. Just as God has mastered our wait, He will give us the words needed to be spoken and will fill us with compassion and love for them. We will hug and hold and kiss and weep! We will thank God and praise God for His faithfulness to protect and return our child. We will celebrate!

Father God is masterful at waiting. There is no prodigal child that He does not wait for, watching to see when they are ready to have His Holy Spirit remind them of their Father's love and care; watching to see when they place their foot on the road home.

CHAPTER 9

There is no day He is too busy to watch for them coming into view on the landscape of wait. Father God stands ready to run to His children, embrace them with love and compassion, and restore them to the center of His family life.

You may be the once-prodigal child who caused another to live in the landscape of wait. The life God gives as we emerge from waiting into the promise is glorious and full. The new life is for both the one waiting and the one waited for. Your family and your Father are eternally thankful you came home.

Coming Home

>I journeyed afar; no thought for Thee,
>Only to find myself in despair and misery.
>Things I sought gave me no reward;
>I was Your prodigal child, renouncing You, Lord.
>In the depths of my shame and waywardness
>There came Your sweet call of love and
>   forgiveness.
>I knelt and prayed with tears of remorse.
>I humbled myself and looked to the Source
>Of love and strength that once I had known.
>My Father God said, "Child, come home!"

APPLICATION:

1. What well-meaning words meant to encourage you have caused you to shout, "Our wait is not your wait!"?

2. Is there any unique situation you need to present to the Lord for instructions in waiting?

3. If a prodigal child has created your wait, what is the most difficult part of your wait? What is your greatest fear?

4. How will you live life well for the Lord, your family, and yourself as you wait?

CHAPTER 10

PRODIGAL WAITING

WE HAVE LOOKED at the predominant figure of the watchful, waiting father in the parable of the prodigal son. This word picture reassures us that our heavenly Father is waiting and watching for the prodigal we love to "come to their senses" and return to our family and to the family of God. We have seen how our Father God allows His earthbound, flesh-framed children to hear deceptive world voices and respond to their call, some ultimately losing all they have received from their Father.

So many of the families you and I know have a beloved prodigal topping their prayer list, one for whom they wait and watch. Some of you, in years past, may have been that prodigal daughter or son. Perhaps you were lured by the false splendor of the world, the false philosophies of postmodern thinkers, or the glitterati of fame and fortune. I don't know how much you "squandered" or where you were when you "came to your spiritual senses." I do know it is an emptiness of spirit, a soul hole that only the Father can fill that gets prodigal children out of the pigsty and headed home.

CHAPTER 10

If the landscape of wait is bleak from the father's perspective until he sees the figure of his son in the distance, then you can be sure the landscape is even bleaker for the prodigal one navigating through it. The further the prodigal travels from the family, the bleaker and longer his landscape of wait. Like a war zone scene, broken dreams and burned-out lives line the roadways. Remnants of what might have been blow like trash across empty lots. The enemy, like the Apostle Peter's roaring lion, prowls, sending the message he or she is captive and will never be able to return home (1 Peter 5:8).

Barbara tells me she watched and waited for her prodigal daughter's return for ten long years. In spite of pain and many disappointments, Barbara never gave up praying for her daughter's return to family and faith.

The wait for the prodigal started when one day that precious child, a self-proclaimed family reject, packed a backpack and headed out to travel across Europe. Barbara told me how her daughter announced in a last meal with the family before her travels that she would be looking for God along the way. One of the visiting grandchildren leaned over and whispered, "Does Auntie know God is right here?"

The hole in her daughter's soul grew larger as her travel experiences added to the weight of sin she carried. She did not find God in any of the places traveled until her last stop, St Paul's Cathedral in London. In the holy hush of a centuries-old sanctuary, God spoke her name, calling her homeward. Barbara's long, prayer-filled wait was finally coming to an end as the glimpse of her daughter on the horizon brought God's promise to fulfillment.

Satan is masterful at convincing some of our children that the values they have learned in our homes, in our churches, and from

God's Word are no longer relevant. He presents a worldview that is 180 degrees from the biblical worldview. He makes right seem wrong and outdated. He makes wrong seem right, a perfect fit for the twenty-first century. As we hear the TV news reports, read the newspaper headlines, and scroll through online news articles, it is evident that much of the world has lost its moral compass. Satan has guided society to redefine words to accommodate his ultimate plan of moral destruction. Jeff Iorg, in his book *Live Like a Missionary*, writes,

> Tolerance has been redefined in this generation. The word formerly meant patience and respect for persons who held positions with which you disagree. Postmodern thought has redefined the word to mean acceptance of every viewpoint as equally valid. Tolerance now means you embrace every ism, tenet, or dogma as true.

Sadly, many of our own children in our families and churches are questioning the Christian values we have lived and taught, buying into the idea that a biblical worldview is wrong because it is not tolerant of all others.

Satan has been at work since Genesis 3, contradicting God's boundaries for our lives, seducing even the best men and women with temptations of what looks good to the eye. When Satan contradicted God's words, "When you eat of it you will surely die" with his lie, "You will not surely die, . . . for God knows that when you eat of it your eyes will be opened, and you will be like God, knowing good and evil," Satan successfully redefined God's words. Adam and Eve, after eating one forbidden fruit, found

CHAPTER 10

themselves hiding in a landscape of wait for God to see their sin and shame. Now they knew Satan for what he truly was and is, a master of evil deceit and seduction. It does not take many bites of forbidden fruit for our children to hide from God, waiting and fearing and knowing He will see their sin and shame.

Isaiah wrote 800 years before Christ, "Woe to those who call evil good and good evil, who put darkness for light and light for darkness, who put bitter for sweet and sweet for bitter" (Isaiah 5:20). The woe of sinful living, the woe of not living with a biblical worldview, results in prodigal children waiting in fear for God to deal with their sin and shame. God will deal with them in a way that reveals their pigsty living, gives them a hunger for the things of the Father, and brings them to their senses.

Out in that landscape of wait and spiritual warfare, the prodigal child comes to a crossroads. Will he take the road marked "Next Week I'll Change," the "After I Get Sober" street, or the avenue of "Let Me Clean Myself Up First"? None of those roads are for the one who has come to his senses. They only lead to more losses and muddier pigsties. The road for them is the one marked "Home" that leads straight to the watching, waiting heavenly Father. There is no beloved child too far gone, too addicted, or too dirty to start down the road called "Home" and find the Father watching and waiting. Barbara's daughter came to her senses. She found both her family and her heavenly Father watching and waiting with joyful anticipation for her return.

Brad is one who serves to shorten the journey for some trying to find their way home. As a volunteer in the local homeless shelter, Street Reach, with its in-house recovery program, Brad leads a weekly Bible study titled *Search for Significance* by Robert McGee. He also facilitates a Christian 12-step program and guides a Relapse to Recovery support group. In our move to South Carolina, we looked for a way to do missions together. We explored a variety of opportunities in our new community: serving meals at the local community kitchen, delivering meals to the homebound, and beginning a home Bible study. None of these gave us what my husband calls a spiritual *aha* moment. It was on our first visit to Street Reach to see if we might serve there when I saw the "aha!" spread across his face. Brad immediately felt a love poured into his heart by God for the men and women sheltered there. Our ministry began with music and a devotional time at the supper meal twice a month.

Recognizing Brad's compassion for the "guests," the director enlisted Brad to begin teaching the *Search for Significance* class. From that first commitment emerged other places of ministry for Brad. From that first night emerged a passion to help addicts and alcoholics hear God's call to new life in Him.

Sadly, some of the men and women we meet at Street Reach are prodigals from families and churches like yours and mine. Lured away by the father of lies, each road they traveled took them deeper into the chemical-using world, introducing them to dependency on drugs and alcohol. They have lost friends, family, jobs, and their integrity as they burned their bridges with lies and abuse. Many have experienced jail time and tried other recovery programs. Years of drug use and alcohol abuse have dulled their senses and begun a slow destruction of body, mind, and soul. Like the prodigal son of Jesus' story, they have squandered everything and found themselves at a pigsty bottom with no one to help.

In their ravaged landscape journey, they have come to their senses and found their way to Street Reach. There they are offered an opportunity to enter the recovery program, where they will experience a healing blend of God's love and personal accountability. Daily, they hear that Jesus has never forgotten them and never stopped loving them. Volunteers like Brad walk with them out of that bleak, war-ravaged landscape down the road to see the Father waiting for their return.

God has called some to leave their comfortable lives and pleasant places to minister in the landscape of wait, to rescue victimized children. In the center of Cumberland, Kentucky, is a restructured building that houses a ministry to children and teenagers. There in that Appalachian Mountains community is Club 180, led by North American Mission Board (NAMB) Mission Service Corps missionaries Terry and Angie Burkeen. They reach out to kids who are victims in the war-torn landscape of wait that is not of their making. Most are born into poverty, abuse, drug- and alcohol-addicted parents, or a combination of all these. They know little about family love or God's love. They search for love and attention in all the wrong places, hoping and waiting for someone to rescue them from painful living. Even before reaching double digits in age, some of these young lives have been seduced by the evil one and have begun to follow the generation before them into the woes of sinful living. Club 180 is a place of refuge, holding out the Jesus lifeline. Terry and Angie tell the true story of their heavenly Father waiting and watching for them to come into the family. They help the children discover that God the Father offers love that will never leave them, never fail them.

If you have a prodigal child, a prodigal sister or brother, or a prodigal grandchild, be encouraged. God has Terrys and Angies and Brads out there to show His redeeming love and guide them on the journey home to you and the heavenly Father. Like Barbara, never give up praying as you wait and watch for their return.

APPLICATION:

1. Who are the prodigals in your life? In the lives of your friends?

2. How can you change your praying to allow God to bring your prodigal to the place where he or she will come to his or her senses?

3. Waiting for the prodigal's return is painful because of the things you know the prodigal is doing and because of the things you imagine happening. God will not waste your pain. He wants to use it. How can you serve the Lord with what He has provided for you in your painful journey through the landscape of wait?

CHAPTER 11

AND IN THE MEANTIME?

YOU HAVE HEARD a promise from God to _____. You fill in the blank. You have begun the journey from the place of hearing God's voice, to His promise-fulfilled destination. It is an eager journey you have set out upon, equipped with God's GPS guiding you along the shortest route from point A to the promised point B. On other journeys with God, you moved efficiently along the highlighted roads. Oh yes, the occasional bump in the road, as my dad called them, slowed your progress at times. An occasional detour was to be expected for some journeys. You navigated them well and were soon back moving swiftly along with the Lord. But this journey is different!

You have watched the green light of God's go change to the yellow light of caution to slow you down. Now the light is red. You have come to a screeching halt. The promise is still far down the road and out of sight. Faithfully, God speaks reassurances as you idle at the red light. You hear and you understand this promise is His promise. It is His to give in His time and in His way. Admit it. Your foot hovers over the pedal, ready to accelerate when the light turns green. That is not the place we want to be in our wait, sitting at a red light, revving the engine in vain. The red light of God's wait turns to green only at His command. Neither the reason for the promise nor the reason for our wait should keep us from participating in the streaming life around us. When God says wait, He usually adds, "And in the meantime!"

The Apostle Paul experienced an "in the meantime" as he waited in Tarsus, modern-day Turkey. Little is known of those silent years, as Bible scholars have coined them. Paul, then called Saul, experienced a life-goal transformation, from persecuting and killing Christians to preaching and proclaiming Jesus is indeed the Christ. His personal experience with the risen Lord set his humble feet on a new road. Because Luke includes Ananias's story of being God's messenger to blind Saul after the Damascus road experience, we can think Saul knew God's assignment for him. God told Ananias in Acts 9:15, "Go! This man is my chosen instrument to proclaim my name to the Gentiles and their kings and to the people of Israel." Acts 9:20 tells us that after his sight returned, "At once he began to preach in the synagogues that Jesus is the Son of God." Saul, soon to be Paul, was on the journey. He had the green light from God.

Early on in Saul's preaching journey he encountered a big bump in the road. God provided Barnabas to help him become part of the apostle team. His new brothers in Christ became the rescue team to help him escape the very persecution he once so diligently administered to Christians. His rescue put him on a long detour road into Tarsus. Once there, the green light of God turned red. What was Paul's meantime?

We don't know the specifics of Paul's silent years. We do know that Paul emerges as God's refined instrument to proclaim Christ's name, the only name whereby man can be saved. Apparently these years are silent only to us, but never were to Paul. Were these years of enlightened study of the Scripture scrolls he loved? Were these years of being molded spiritually and physically to endure great hardship for his Lord: beatings, shipwreck, imprisonment? Were these years of sharing Jesus and seeing friends and family of Tarsus come to Father God through Christ the Son? How can our *meantime* be as refining and as preparing as Paul's?

If Paul were alive today, I would describe him in twenty-first-century terms: *driven, innovative, strong, highly intellectual, and a champion of Jesus;* also *missional, relational, adventuresome, a detailed journal writer,* and *one deeply devoted to all things Christ.* I wonder if in his postconversion silent years, Paul meditated on the words of David's Psalm 37:7, "Be still before the Lord and wait patiently for Him"? *Still. Waiting. Patiently.* None of these words made my top ten descriptors for Paul. David wrote from an experiential understanding of wait, words that have calmed God's people for thousands of years as they wait for God's promises. Perhaps the soothing words of David's pastoral psalms were a balm to Paul as he waited. We, too, can let the beautiful hymns and praise songs written from these psalms flow through our hearts to soothe our impatient souls in the meantime of waiting.

I am not a still person by nature. I cannot sit quietly in front of the television simply watching the screen. I will always have my hands and mind busy with a crossword puzzle, a sudoku, or a piece of handwork. I will think of something that needs to be done and will immediately get up to do it. On the other hand, I can spend hours in a book that captivates my mind, or walk for miles on country lanes or along the seashore. But to stop and be at a standstill is not my nature. Yet God brings it to us through David in a commanding way. "Be still"; "Quiet down"; "Rest in the

CHAPTER 11

Lord" are the several translations we read for this verse. Friends and family are quick to advise you with these words. I heard it often, too often. I read the verse and underlined it in red. I wonder now if Paul grew more still when he underlined scroll verses in red first-century ink. This verse can stand alone, but to understand the full command of God we must look back. Verse 7 is in the top left column of my Bible when I open it and turn to Psalms. So it was not until I turned back the page to read the previous four verses that understanding came to me.

> *Trust in the LORD and do good; dwell in the land and enjoy safe pasture. Delight yourself in the LORD and he will give you the desires of your heart. Commit your way to the LORD; trust in him and he will do this: He will make your righteousness shine like the dawn, the justice of your cause like the noonday sun. Be still before the LORD and wait patiently for him* (Psalm 37:3–7).

Stillness in the wait is not physical; it is spiritual. Can you say yes with me? This soul realization of spiritual stillness brings to our heart the issue of trust once again. To continue our journey analogy in this chapter, trust is posted throughout the landscape of wait like mile markers on our interstate highways. When God says *wait* as you journey with Him, spiritual stillness comes only through trust in the Lord.

Trust does not stand alone, though, in David's words of commands from God to us. Trust is partnered with "do good." Together they proceed, "dwell in the land and enjoy safe pasture." I looked around in my wait and did not want to have to do anything there, much less stop and dwell there. That was not the promised place and it did not look pastoral to my promise-focused eyes. *Pastoral* is about pleasant places where happiness and fulfillment are found, where sheep graze contentedly on gently sloping hillsides. How do we wrap our minds around this to be spiritually still in our wait?

David took seriously and experientially the Word of God to Joshua who led the Israelites generations before: "Keep this Book of the Law always on your lips; meditate on it day and night, so that you may be careful to do everything written in it. Then you will be prosperous and successful" (Joshua 1:8). Not knowing we would need a key to His beautiful words of trust and stillness before God, David was led by God to provide the key in Psalm 1:2, words that echo God's words to Joshua. "Meditate on it day and night." David, a master at meditating, writes that this is his delight, meditating on God's law. It can be our delight, too, if we would take a page or a psalm from David's book and make it our own. In fact, take several. In the NIV Bible there are 16 psalms that speak to meditating on the things of God: on His promises, His law, His goodness, His love, His mighty deeds, His commands, His statutes, and His unfailing love. Choose one to delight in today and tonight and the next day and night.

I think we are getting the true pastoral picture now. Our safe pasture will be wherever God stops us along the way. We will not simply rest in the safe pasture, but we will be nurtured and blessed to serve and do good to others along the way. As Brad and I waited to move south, we obediently stepped aside from our many church and denominational responsibilities one by one. For each and every place we had served, God provided someone to step into our shoes. God used our wait to help train them in

CHAPTER 11

financial skills, deacon responsibilities, stewardship knowledge, WMU leadership skills, and nurse management. We found a full measure of doing good in our stop on the journey of wait.

Our decision to leave a lifetime of family and friends in New England was not well understood. Some boldly said they were praying our home would not sell. Others actually voiced fear at being called by God to go someplace else, anyplace else. We understood that. As time wore on in our wait, we found new encouragement from friends who now saw the whole picture—the call of God, the journey with God, the wait for God, and the fulfillment by God. They spoke of hoping they would be able to be faithful to a call from God like ours and spoke of our faithful waiting as inspiring.

APPLICATION:

1. Where did you experience the red light of stop from God?

2. Make a list of hymns and praise songs about being still or at rest before the Lord.

3. What have you found applicable from Paul's silent years?

4. Choose a psalm on which to meditate today and tonight.

5. What is your "in the meantime" of doing good that God has for you in your wait?

CHAPTER 12

THE WAY OF GOD'S SURPRISE

MEDICAL MISSIONS PROMISED to be a major piece of my early retirement. Years of family practice nursing prepared me to fit well into a variety of missions team settings. I was certain God's call to retire was a call to use my nursing this way. The world would become my nursing clinic setting. A year into life with our new church family, a construction missions team formed. It needed a medical coordinator. No hand went up faster than mine for this assignment. With another nurse I shared the responsibility to keep our construction team hydrated and take care of medical needs, while our team built a concrete-block house in a few short days in Piedras Negras, Mexico.

The health of a team is critical to completion of a missions team's purpose. On that first missions trip, I learned about the importance of the medical coordinator's role. Having organized the medical staff and the work of nurses in a large family practice, I was challenged to create a comprehensive plan for missions team medical coordinators. Following the trip that focused on building a house out of concrete blocks—but that did not share Christ in concrete ways with the family—several of us were hopeful that God would one day return us to Mexico for opportunities to intentionally share Christ with the lost.

As much as I enjoyed serving as medical coordinator, my desire was to use my nursing skills with people who needed to know Jesus. Holding on to the promise that God's plan for retirement would include medical missions, I waited patiently for the door to open. Our church began to expand its missions vision and look for ways to partner in missions with our Southern Baptist missionaries. Our pastor presented me with the opportunity to participate in a vision trip sponsored by Appalachian Regional Ministries to visit sites where our North American Mission Board (NAMB) missionaries were serving. Everything in me wanted to say, *Yes! I'll go!* The Spirit of God was saying to me, *Not you, Debby.* I could not understand. My response was less than humble. *Not me? I am the WMU director. Really? Not me, Lord?* I cast about in my mind with the thought, *If not me, who?* I prayed about it and the Lord directed me to Bill and Gloria Stubbs as the ones He wanted to go on that tour. They were reluctant but willing to go. Gloria confided in me that she would go, but not to expect her to return to lead subsequent missions trips. Bill told me he was only going to keep Miss Gloria safe.

Bill and Gloria climbed aboard the motor coach and settled back to enjoy the mountain scenery, the companionship of other travelers, and to bring a report back to our church staff of possible missions connections. Along the way, in their stop in the mountains of eastern Kentucky, God made a personal connection for them. He broke their hearts for the missions work of Meridzo Ministries and the hardscrabble life of the people in the once-booming coal mining tricities of Lynch, Benham, and Cumberland, Kentucky.

Compassion moved them to return with a report of immense potential for partnering with our missionaries there.

The report our church received included Bill and Gloria's recommendation to create a partnership with our missionaries there, and the desire to lead the first missions team. Their report sounded as if a medical team would be a perfect fit for those very poor communities. As plans were being made and the team was filling with volunteers (which included me) Gloria communicated with the missionaries, at my urging, about the possibility of a medical component. There was no response. The team would do construction work, prayerwalk, visit the homebound and a nursing home, and work at the clothing center. All good, none needing a nurse. All good, but not using the skills I hoped to use for Jesus there.

Various responsibilities were assigned and small teams formed for the various projects. I would lead the prayerwalking team each morning. I *will* do missions outside of that which has a medical focus. One of our church staff has accused me of getting excited about *any* kind of missions anywhere. He is correct. Anywhere and by any means that Jesus is presented to the lost is exciting and I am thankful to be part of it! In fact, on most of the missions teams, I have had less opportunity to participate in nursing and have had more involvement in everything else.

Prayerwalking is a natural fit for me. When I walk my neighborhood, I pray for the families in the homes I pass, lifting their names to the Father as I read them on the mailboxes; lifting any needs I discern from my observations and conversations along the way. From my first experience learning the fundamentals of prayerwalking from author and prayerwalker Randy Sprinkle more than 20 years ago, to coordinating prayerwalking in towns

CHAPTER 12

and cities from New England to Hawaii, prayerwalking has predominated missions for me.

On our first Monday morning in Kentucky, as teams were gathering to pray and go out to their assigned tasks, a woman rushed in and loudly asked if anyone with us was a nurse. All eyes turned to me, sharing my immediate thought that there must be a medical emergency and I was the logical one in the group to respond. In full nurse mode I calmly responded with, "What has happened?" Introducing herself as the local medical team coordinator (we didn't know she and her position even existed), she told us a dental team had arrived the previous night without their nurse. Without a nurse to examine patients and determine they were medically able to have dental care, the clinic could not be held. When the dental team's nurse fell ill at the last moment and could not go, the team prayed. God told them to go, for He would provide the nurse in Lynch, Kentucky. My prayerwalking team all said, "Go, Debby!"

With stethoscope and Bible in hand, I was thrust into the surprise of God in my wait for using my nursing in missions. Without notice, but in God's perfect timing, my skills were needed. Who am I, who are any of us, that God must reveal the time and way for Him to set us down in His place of promise? When the time comes, it will meet a need that is bigger than any plans we can make. For four days I met with more than 100 local men, women, and children coming to the little, brick church where the dentist set up his equipment. I took a medical history, did appropriate predental work exams, and listened to their dental needs. Nearly everyone I talked with was open to spiritual conversations. Scriptures, prayer, and even tears were part of my responses to their confidences about family needs and their own deep soul needs. Those many witnessing opportunities were direct from God's heart to each heart I listened to with physical and spiritual ears.

When God seems to be disallowing what appears to you to be exactly right, when every means to discovering a way to reach His promise has no results, it could mean God wants to surprise you. We don't have to worry if we will be properly equipped when the surprise moment arrives. Jesus sent His disciples out carrying little (Luke 9:3). My Bible and stethoscope were all I needed to do God's spiritual and nursing work that week. We don't have to worry if we will have the words to say. God's heart spoke to my heart with the right words for each patient. What joy I experienced sharing the love of Christ with so many! What joy I experienced, not simply for providing nursing, but because I again experienced our God's faithfulness to keep His promise and experienced the way of God's surprise.

Oswald Chambers wrote in *My Utmost for His Highest* a devotional thought on the Scripture verse, "Nevertheless not my will, but thine, be done" (Luke 22:42). "God sometimes allows you to get into a place of testing where your own welfare would be the right and proper thing to consider; but if you are living the life of faith, you will joyfully waive your right and leave God to choose for you."

If I had not waived my right to being on the vision trip through Appalachian Regional Ministries and offered it to Gloria and Bill, and if I had not waived what seemed right for me, I would not have been free to participate in this first medical missions assignment from God. My heart may not have been broken for the needy in that place. My mind may not have grasped any mission site in that trip as a connection for our church. I would

CHAPTER 12

have missed the surprise of God in my wait. We must be sensitive to God's leading, not our own leading; to God's will, not our own. Promises kept by God do not necessarily herald in a new lifestyle or a new missions work. In this case, medical missions did not become the focus of missions for me. As our church partnered with Lynch, Kentucky, and then began a partnership with missionaries along the Gulf Coast of Mexico, I continued to look for God's nod for medical missions.

Neil Trask, a local cardiologist, is a deep man of God. Every time I was with him, I felt God at work in his heart. At one point, I asked him if he would consider medical missions. To my usual spate of many enthusiastic words of missions ideas he responded with reluctance, saying he did not see himself as a potential missions team volunteer. I know better than to try to do the Holy Spirit's work. I was responsible to plant the mission seed. God would water it. Some seeds sprout quickly with a little watering and fertile soil. The seed sown in Neil for missions took a little longer, but not a day longer than God's timing for our first medical missions team. Neil arrived at a place where the Spirit's call could not be denied. He came to me and said he was ready to say, "Yes, Lord!" to medical missions. I was singing hallelujah!

Doug and Darla Millar, our missionaries in Mexico with whom we were now connecting, had recently begun a ministry in a remote Mayan village in Central Mexico. The clusters of little houses made from sticks with grass roofs were without running water or electricity. This would be our church's first medical team destination. In a short time, God put together a team of four physicians, two nurses, a physician's assistant, a public health educator, a dental hygienist, our pastor, and a geologist. Is the geologist part not a fit in your mind? Forrest actually became the go-to guy for everything not medical! This worked perfectly. Every team needs a go-to person like this.

For Jennifer, our dental hygienist, this was her first missions trip. Jennifer grew up in Girls in Action® (GA®) and Acteens® at a church not too far from our church in Myrtle Beach. As a young GA at Camp LaVida, she heard God's call to missions. This first missions trip to Mexico and the subsequent yearly missions trips Jennifer has made when a GA have been her "Yes, Lord!" to His call to missions. Jennifer didn't know yes to God would include the grayest teeth she had ever cleaned or the presence of tarantulas on the ceiling above her as she transformed gray teeth to pearly white. Jennifer's heart had been shaped in missions education to say yes to God wherever He took her, no matter what conditions she found. Jennifer spent six to eight long hours cleaning teeth for Jesus on each clinic day.

This was Dr. Jim's first missions trip. As the senior member of the team and the only family practitioner in the group, it would be his expertise in everyday medical issues we relied upon. One of the first patients who arrived at our clinic was a woman in her 30s. Her body language spoke of great sadness. Through two translators, her story of bleeding for four years emerged. Through tears she spoke of her husband rejecting her, her children not

CHAPTER 12

respecting her, and her village having no use for her because she was too tired to do the work women do in her village. Hugging her stooped shoulders, I told her that God knew her problem and He did not reject her. He loved her and had sent us here to tell her about Him and His Son Jesus, and to bring her some help. I knew she would need more physical care than we could give her. We could not do the surgery she needed to fully correct the bleeding.

I took her to see Dr. Jim. After reviewing her story and talking more about her symptom, he told her about the medicine he would give her to help ease the bleeding and make her feel better. He then told her about a woman just like her who had bled for 12 years, a woman just like her who was rejected by her family and her village, and who, like her, made her way through a crowd to touch the hem of Jesus' robe to perhaps find a miracle of healing. Dr. Jim then used an evangelism picture cube to share the gospel of Jesus through two translators—English to Spanish and Spanish to Mayan. She told Dr. Jim, "I want to know your Jesus." Dr. Jim was overjoyed by this opportunity to share Jesus through medical missions.

That week I watched God transform our team from professional urban Christian health-care givers to a team of missions-hearted men and women taking every opportunity to share Jesus with lost, hurting, primitive-living people for whom Christ died. They became a team that allowed God to take them to the next level of living utterly devoted missional lives for their Lord.

Waiting for God does not have to be a bleak landscape. It can be the place for putting all the pieces together—the pieces of needed skills, the piece of the right place, the piece of the right people—so when God's timing is right, all is in place.

APPLICATION:

1. Describe a promised place to serve in which the Lord has required a wait.

2. What must you release of God's leading to another, setting aside what seems right for you?

3. How has God surprised you in a wait to serve Him?

4. How have you said "Yes, Lord!" for missions?

5. What pieces are you seeing come together for God's promise to be fulfilled?

CHAPTER 13

BATTLES IN THE WAIT

BATTLES AND WARS—SCRIPTURE tells the story of battles won and lost, wars waged, and kingdoms conquered. History timelines are marked by dates of wars waged between tribes and nations. Every generation has listened to war stories told around the dinner table by parents and grandparents. As three generations of my family gathered around our dinner table, I heard stories of my grandfather's service in World War I in the infantry in France and of my dad's World War II navy service in the Pacific. Usually their conversations ended with discussion over which war was the "Big War." Underlying their congenial comparison of stories was a guarded sense of miraculous survival amid fierce battles. My grandfather was severely wounded while on a scouting mission and ultimately lost a leg. Dad was a corpsman assigned to the first marine division invasion of the island of Okinawa, surviving the enemy machine gun fire as men fell around him.

Every family's story of war includes a chapter of waiting for their warrior to return home. Figuring large in this wait is the face of a woman waiting for her soldier. She is waiting for her husband, her son, or her fiancé to return to her. When war comes, those who love the soldiers, the sailors, the airmen, and the marines enter a landscape of wait. Those who are followers of the Lord Jesus can say with the psalmist, "We wait in hope for the Lord; He is our help and our shield" (Psalm 33:20).

Fighting the Battle with Patience and Faith

Eiblis is a woman familiar with this landscape of wartime wait. In 1969 her fiancé, Teddy, was sent to the jungles of Vietnam to join the infantry ground troops for a one-year tour of duty. As the wait for Teddy's return began, Eiblis heard a promise from God for his safe return. She would cling to this promise through the long days and nights, clutching her crucifix under her pillow each night as she prayed, "Dear Lord, keep him safe and bring him home." Deeply in love with her soldier, she describes this year of war separation as a "true test of faith." As the days dragged by, and pages slowly turned on the calendar, Eiblis discovered a new depth to her faith in God. Unshakeable faith in Christ was emerging to guard and guide her wait.

In the days before technology enabled deployed soldiers to communicate frequently by email and to see their beloved's faces on Skype, Eiblis and Teddy communicated solely by letter writing through the long 12 months of his Vietnam tour of duty. The most frightening day in all her days of wait, she recounts, was 10 months into her wait, when she thought she could no longer recall the sound of Teddy's voice. Through 2 more long months, Eiblis strained to remember the tones and inflections of Teddy's voice. On the day of his return, the immediate recognition of his voice was the "Yes, Lord!" to her faith.

Eiblis credits the example of her parents' strong faith as foundational to her deepening faith in her wait. She watched their faith tested many times as they clothed, fed, and educated eight children. Their life tests never weakened their faith, but instead served to strengthen their faith in, as her father would say, "the good Lord who would never let them down." So, too, has it been for Eiblis and Teddy over time.

When Teddy was diagnosed with esophageal cancer five years ago, Eiblis was thrust into another landscape of wait, but one she and Teddy would navigate together. This would be a new war, with many battles in which they would engage an unseen but relentless enemy. Every conversation I have had with Eiblis in the years since his diagnosis, surgery, and several chemotherapy stretches has revealed her faith in the good Lord who will not let them down. When the surgeon came to speak to her before the surgery, she took his hands and prayed, asking God to bless his hands. The surgeon was amazed, saying no one had ever done that. In the waiting room with her four adult children around her, Eiblis stood through Teddy's 13-hour radical surgery, standing in faith and in silent prayer as the surgeon stood operating on her husband. Again God returned Teddy to her from a place of great danger and looming death as she waited in faith for her man to return.

Their battle for health is not over. This war against cancer has not ended. Nearly five years free of cancer, metastatic tumors developed. Teddy continues on a chemotherapy regimen that has shrunk the tumors and given him and Eiblis more chapters to write in their life story. Faith in the every-moment presence of God enables them to journey with the joy of life, even in the shadow of death, through this landscape of wait.

CHAPTER 13

"The LORD has heard my cry for mercy; the LORD accepts my prayer" (Psalm 6:9). Eiblis has lived out this verse believing God indeed hears our cries and accepts our prayers as we wait for His promises.

You may be the woman or man waiting on the home front for a warrior to return. Or you may be one walking through a landscape of wait scarred not by missiles and bombs but by disease and surgery and therapy. Take heart, my sisters and brothers. Our Lord hears your cries for mercy and accepts your prayers for every battle waged. Psalm 121:4 reminds us, "Indeed, He who watches over Israel will neither slumber nor sleep." The Lord God Almighty is alert to hear every prayer you bring to Him, be it midday or midnight.

As you bring your cries for mercy and your prayers to the Lord, let these words of David in Psalm 27:14 give you holy advice for battle landscapes of wait. "Wait for the LORD; be strong and take heart and wait for the LORD." *The Message* paraphrase gives us the idea of not only waiting but staying in the wait. "Stay with God! Take heart. Don't quit. I'll say it again: Stay with God." The joy of waiting for God is the reality we are actually with God in the wait. God is not simply observing us from far away in heaven's throne room. He is with us by His Holy Spirit who indwells us as followers of Jesus. The presence of God is palpable and personal in the wait for the promise we have heard from God.

At Peace in the Battle

Nina and Swami have navigated the disease-ridden landscape of wait to discover the faithfulness of God and confirm the trustworthiness of His promises. Crohn's disease has been a challenge for Swami for many years, but has been well-managed most of the time. Occasionally symptoms would worsen but then be brought back under control. When symptoms flared up again in 2001, they were presumed to be part of his Crohn's disease. This time, tests revealed cancer. Their world tilted.

Nina, a woman of deep faith, immediately went to her church to pray. On her knees, in the presence of the Lord, she poured out her heart and asked God for a word of promise. As her hands turned the pages of her Bible and her eyes scanned the Scriptures through her tears, God led her to this promise in Psalm 27:13, "I am still confident of this: I will see the goodness of the Lord in the land of the living." With these words of promise Nina and Swami journeyed confidently through the landscape of wait together to find the goodness of the Lord in the land of the living.

Weeks of chemotherapy and radiation prepared the way for Swami's surgery. During this time, Nina shouldered more responsibility in their home and in their business. Still, she made time to stay in the Word, participating in a Bible study focusing on women in the Bible. Prompted by the Holy Spirit, Nina asked the Lord, *Who am I? With which of these women do I relate?* God revealed to her it was Priscilla.

Priscilla and her husband, Aquila, were contemporaries of the Apostle Paul. He described them as "fellow workers in Christ Jesus" (Romans 16:3). This was not the direction Nina hoped for. Priscilla's name was most often listed before Aquila's name. Not wanting to be the leader in their marriage, Nina waited for God to show her more. God told her that for this season of their life, she would have to shoulder more responsibility, but not forever. Further study revealed when this biblical couple is first met, Aquila is listed first. In 1 Corinthians, Aquila is again listed first, a time when a church has begun to meet in their home. Nina

CHAPTER 13

claimed the example of Priscilla and Aquila as a second God-given promise for Swami's restoration to again lead their home and business.

Two strong promises from God gave great strength for the wait. Each time a new challenge or a setback was encountered, Nina would draw strength from them and remind the Lord of His promises saying, "You said! You said, Lord!"

The third promise came through their son Kyle. A teenager at the time of his dad's cancer treatment, Kyle already held a focal point in his mother's prayers, not unlike most teenagers on their mothers' hearts. Nina had been praying that the Spirit of the Lord would be on Kyle, that he would hear God speak to him through dreams as described in Joel 2:28. God brought the third promise to Kyle in a dream. His dream was of their swimming pool, an older pool in need of repair. But in his dream it was filled with clean, clear water. His father stood in the middle of it with a family friend who was giving him swimming instructions. Nina tells me Swami did not swim, only going into the pool to play with the children when they were young. This beautiful dream of newness and of life blessed and strengthened Nina, Kyle, and Swami for their wait for promised healing.

Not all journeys through the journey of wait for promised healing ends with perfect health in this life. Some, like my friends Sherry, Ed, and Pat, found their healing as they entered heaven's gate and were greeted by the Great Physician. Not all journeys end with a return home and resumption of living the routines of life, never to be interrupted again. Eiblis and Teddy continue to battle cancer. Nina and Swami were thrust back into an even bleaker landscape when Swami developed a bowel blockage and a subsequent gall bladder rupture.

The once-optimistic faces of the doctors and surgeons were now guarded with the gravity of the situation. Nina's heart broke again in the retelling of praying over Swami as he prepared for surgery to try to save his life. The doctors told her to prepare for the worst. There was little hope the surgery would be successful because of the fragility of the tissue from the impact of past chemotherapy and radiation. Nina boldly reminded God of His promise to their family to restore their father. But with those words, the Spirit of God came over her, requiring total submission to God's will for their lives. Nina submitted her will to God's will, placed Swami in His care, and prayed, "If you are ready for him, I am ready, God."

Nina faced a crisis of faith in that moment. She did not shy away from the possibility that it was God's will for Swami to find healing in heaven by Jesus' side and not hers. She took heart, waited for the Lord to bring healing to Swami according to His perfect will in the perfect place. God chose to bring healing through successful surgery and enabling his tender tissues to hold the needed suturing. Nina and Swami are living in the joy of fulfilled promises and the experience of total submission to the lordship of Jesus Christ.

We wish life could be free of the emotional and physical battle scars of war. We hope that our lives would escape battling the ravages of cancer, heart disease, and other life-compromising medical conditions, but in this life there will be battles on many fronts. It is in the fire of battle that our God refines us. For Nina and Eiblis, in their wait for healing, love for their husbands has grown stronger, their love for their Lord God deeper.

APPLICATION:

1. How has God been a shield to you in your wait for a soldier, sailor, airman, or marine to return from war?

2. *Unshakeable faith!* Can this be applied to your waiting situation? Explain.

3. How will you "take heart" and "stay with God" according to Psalm 27?

4. Describe your Scripture search for promises from God for your wait.

5. What lessons from Eiblis and Nina will you apply to your own journey through the landscape of wait during your own or someone you love's battle for health?

CHAPTER 14

WAITING AT THE WELL

WELLS IN OLD and New Testament days marked property ownership by families, cities, and nations. Wells were the source of life-giving water for people and for their livestock. Wells were the meeting place for communities and a stopping place for those journeying through the area. One might look back through Scripture at well story settings and find significant waits by people on whom God had His hand; find wellside divine appointments with God.

Abraham's servant, sent to find a wife for Isaac, finished his journey to Abraham's homeland to wait by a well. Moses, having fled from Pharaoh, stops at a well and rescues a fair maiden who soon becomes his wife.

Wells that had lost their spring water sources were used as means of imprisonment and slow death. Joseph's life was changed when his brothers, meaning evil for him, put him in a dry well. But God meant good for Him, delivered him from a well wait and put him on an incredible journey of faith and serving in a far-off land. Jeremiah was another man of God sentenced to well waiting but delivered to continue serving God.

CHAPTER 14

In Genesis 16 we find Hagar, the first recorded exploited woman of the Bible, sitting by a well along a desert road to Shur. Hagar was an Egyptian servant of Sarah and Abraham. She was promoted from maid for Sarah to wife of Abraham so a child could be conceived, their family begun, and the promise of God manipulated to be fulfilled. This ill-conceived plan brought both conception and contention in Abraham's household. Pregnant Hagar fled the mistreatment by Sarah and arrived at the well where life would be changed.

Have you wondered why Hagar was waiting at the well? Was it for someone to help her draw water, having fled from Sarah on foot with only what she could carry? Was it to find another traveler headed to Egypt, her homeland, with whom it would be safe for a woman to travel? Was it perhaps the advancement of pregnancy that wearied her until she could not proceed one step more? Or was it an unexplainable sense that this was the place where both refreshing water and refreshing hope for her future would be found? While waiting at the well, the angel of the Lord found Hagar.

This conversation began with questions to Hagar, whose answers were already known by the angel of the Lord. More so, already known were the circumstances that brought her to the well and the fears she harbored for her unborn child. He went straight to the heart of these matters, partnering instructions with promises. A dramatic change came to Hagar. She identified this angelic messenger as God. Hagar was the first person to give a name for God—*El Roi,* "the God who sees me" (Genesis 16:13). Hagar in turn partnered the reality of God seeing her with the statement, "I have now seen the One who sees me." In newness of faith, she returned to Abraham and Sarah.

Waiting at the Well in Samaria

The angel of the Lord visited the ancient well on the road to Shur. The Son of God visited Jacob's well on the road through Samaria. As John 4 tells it, at this first-century well, the eyes of El Roi, "the God who sees," focused on another exploited woman, the Samaritan woman. She came to the well after the village women had probably finished drawing their daily water. Perhaps she came at a later time to avoid her neighbors, who looked with scorn on her because of her multiple marriages and current living in sin arrangement. We don't know the cause of her spiraling down and away from right living into an adulterous relationship. What we do know from the story is that she was weary of not just toting daily water but of carrying the shame of wrong life choices.

Jesus began their conversation with a focus on water, moves to the reality of her life situation, responded to her attempt to change the subject, and then stunningly revealed Himself as Messiah, the source of Living Water, who would quench her true thirst.

As Christ followers, we never tire of this story of divine appointments with Jesus, of Living Water statements of truth, and of hope offered to the cast down and the cast outs. As Christ followers we are challenged to cross barriers to share the eternal life-giving gospel message with Jesus' least of these. Whenever the Divine meets disgrace, transformation results.

Look at the parallels in these two God-seeing meetings. Both women were in a landscape of wait that seems endless and hopeless. Both women were filled with the shame and frustrations of their life situations. Both women took to the road: one took to the road and ran away; one trudged the same road every day in an ever-deepening rut. Both women's journeys through the landscape of wait ended at a well.

Both women were questioned, but the truth of their life situations was already well known to the Lord at the well. Both women, who had life defined by others and had been misused by them, came face-to-face with the only One who could rescue and give them hope. Both women came to the well for water for that day's need, hoping to remain unseen. Both found the eyes of the Lord focused on them and a promise for all the days of their lives.

We cannot be Christ followers and not stop at wells of wait along our way. John writes that Jesus had to go through Samaria. Great hindsight on John's part! Traveling back to Galilee with Jesus, John just didn't get it when Jesus took the road through Samaria, crossing religious barriers. Nor did he get it when after going into the town to get food, they returned to find Jesus crossing social barriers, talking with a woman (and such a woman). He didn't get it when Jesus crossed physical barriers, no longer hungry but saying, "My food is to do the will of Him who sent me and to finish His work." This statement of Jesus begs the question, *Is my food, is my sustenance doing the will of Him who sends me to do His kingdom work?* Perhaps that question came to John's mind as he, the beloved disciple, saw Jesus' love extended to the woman at the well.

The sustenance Jesus spoke of was the spiritual sustenance that comes from being in the will of God to do the will of God. Like the disciples, we, too, at times just don't get it—don't get that to be a follower of Jesus we must be like Jesus, doing what God gives us to do and going where He leads us to go. Living for Jesus would be easy if it meant keeping to ourselves, staying within our religious and social self-imposed barriers, staying inside our safe churches to mingle only with proper believers. If Jesus delighted in the spiritual food of doing the Father's will beyond barriers set by religion and society, then as Christ followers, we, too will find great delight in the food served beyond the barriers. To find it we must sometimes go through Samaria.

Going Through Samaria

Samaria represents the dreaded, difficult places to go. These are the places where your past pain, private fears, and personal prejudices strive to keep you from saying with Jesus, "I must go through Samaria." In these dark landscapes of wait are wells by which someone is waiting to be seen, and known, and offered Living Water. Is it to work at a well with alcoholics and addicts to show them a way out of their addictions to dependency on Christ? Is it to minister to parents grieving over children they have lost in death, to reveal the Christ comforter for broken hearts? Is it to go past the locked gates and iron bars of prisons where you or someone you love has been incarcerated, to bring spiritual freedom in the name of Jesus? Is it to rescue women, girls, and boys caught in the tangled web of human exploitation like you once were or your precious daughter is now? Or is it to allow the harsh memories of war experiences to spur you on to help wounded warriors returning from today's battlefronts? God does not waste your pain. He wants to use it for His glory!

As a couple, Brad and I have turned to Oswald Chambers's *My Utmost for His Highest* for devotional guidance. A favorite selection is,

> At times God puts us through the discipline of darkness to teach us to heed Him. Song birds

CHAPTER 14

> are taught to sing in the dark, and we are put into the shadow of God's hand until we learn to hear Him. . . . Watch where God puts you into darkness, and when you are there keep your mouth shut. Are you in the dark just now in your circumstances, or in your life with God? Then remain quiet. . . . When you are in the dark, listen, and God will give you a very precious message for someone else when you get into the light.

What precious message of hope will you carry into the dark places of wait from your place of light?

Brad and I have been successfully transplanted by God's ever-sufficient grace from New Hampshire's rocky coastline to South Carolina's sandy beaches. It is a simple matter to transplant a young seedling. Good soil, the right proportions of sun and rain, and soon a tree grows tall and strong. But when you transplant a mature tree, there is no guarantee that it will thrive in its new setting, even in perfect conditions. That old tree liked where it was. It offered its shade there. In the new place, it just wants to wither and die. But when God by His grace shakes the tree, loosens the soil, and pulls up the roots, the old tree is amazingly freed to live, and grow, and produce fruit in its new place. So it has been for us in South Carolina. Now we sip sweet tea, enjoy our shrimp on grits, and want y'all to come back and visit.

Me and My Well of Samaria

In chapter 10 you read about Brad serving at the local shelter and leading groups in the alcohol and addictions recovery program.

There is another chapter in our story of serving there. I confess to being a bit uncomfortable the first night we visited, mingling with the unwashed and unhealthy and greeting the resident addicts and alcoholics in the program. When Brad announced in the car on the way home, "This is the place *we* are to serve," I nearly blurted out what I was thinking, *Not me*. The peace of God, the will of God, was hovering all around his big, smiling face. I was not feeling peace and definitely not smiling. I did not want to revisit the pain experienced when our family faced the ravages of alcoholism and addictions. Carefully hiding my reaction, I agreed to volunteer with him for the mission services two nights a month.

Brad's love for the men and women who came in each night, and his joy in each man and woman in the program working on a spiritual journey to sobriety and staying clean, were evident. God was not only working in their lives at the mission, He was working on me. The love of Christ for each one there was being poured into my heart. A peace for serving with those at this modern-day Samaritan well was emerging.

In time, I heard a quiet voice calling to me, "What about the women?" Fearing where this question might take me, I tentatively asked Brad what the women had that was just for them. "Nothing! Yet!" he answered. A week later the program director called me in for a little visit, saying she "just wanted to get to know me." Thinking she might have been prompted to this invitation, I was a little leery. She shared her desire to have a Bible study for the women, helping them not only be sober and clean, but to become godly women. I cautiously joined in the conversation, saying if she wanted that for the women, they needed a woman to teach them. I suggested she consider a study about women in the Bible.

CHAPTER 14

She had a funny smile on her face as I agreed to pray with her for someone to do this.

You have probably surmised God led me to discover my food was to do the will of God there in my Samaria. As the new ladies Bible study began, we focused week by week on various women of the Bible. Over the next six years I watched God's Holy Word penetrate the drug-and-alcohol-induced fog of countless women as they became children of God and began to lead godly lives. I experienced the delight of being in the will of God and doing His will. God transforms us when we finally say with Jesus, "I must go through Samaria."

APPLICATION:

1. Is there a well at which you have waited for someone to see you, really see you? A well where someone would hear your heart's cry and give you a promise?

2. Is there a well to which you have trudged day after day carrying the shame of your past and your present, hoping the future could be transformed?

3. Are there wells where someone you care about is waiting, waiting for change but not knowing the One who can bring change and give them new life?

CHAPTER 14

4. What pain have you endured, what heartache have you borne that God wants to use at a well where someone waits to meet Jesus? Where is your Samaria?

5. Describe the love God has poured into you for those you minister to at the wells of wait.

CHAPTER 15

CROSSROADS OF WAIT

JOURNEYING THROUGH THE landscape of wait we find not only wells along the side of the road, but also numerous crossroads. Drawing near, we hope for signs of personal direction posted by the hand of God. We pray for a Holy Spirit-guided GPS to mark our way and point out the route. Which road should we take to reach our promised destination? Should we venture straight across? Make a left turn across the path of oncoming pilgrims in hopes of finding a shorter, safer route? Make a quick right turn on a new road that could be a dead end? More importantly, how do we see God's signposts directing us onto the right road?

Scripture addresses these crossroads questions. Jeremiah 6:16 tells us, "This is what the LORD says: 'Stand at the crossroads and look; ask for the ancient paths, ask where the good way is, and walk in it, and you will find rest for your souls.'"

Waiting for God is more about moving forward, more about walking through its landscape toward promise than about standing still, bogged down in the mire. Because of this, crossroads of decision making will be encountered. In the early days of HGTV

CHAPTER 15

programs promising immediate results by "staging" your home to sell, our realtor gave us several options that she thought would bring us a buyer and secure a new home. I have mentioned that new carpets, bridge loans, and buried icons were a few of the ideas posed to us. This intersection of decision making in our wait gave us opportunity to stand at the crossroads and look, to ask God what His good and ancient path was, and to choose to walk in it.

God's path for us was straight ahead along the road leading to "rest for your souls." No left turn to recarpet the house, no right turn to the dead end of burying icons in the front yard, and definitely no U-turns across a bridge loan over a river of debt. As we stood at this crossroads, Brad recognized our intersection was not just of roads to travel, but more importantly of words for witnessing. Sitting at our realtor's desk, Brad spoke of our promise from God, our understanding of God keeping us in New Hampshire for this time of wait, and of our complete trust in Jesus who was directing every step of the journey. His words were perhaps not ones she had heard before from clients. Our initial eagerness to sell our home and move south did not fit with our unwillingness to do whatever it took to sell. Incomprehension was evident on her face, a reaction we would see on other faces as we waited for God's timing.

We chose to walk in the way God had set for us, the ancient path of trust and obedience through a landscape of wait. A. W. Tozer said,

> "For not only does sound reason direct us to refuse the guidance of those who do or teach anything wrong, but it is by all means vital for

the lover of truth, regardless of the threat of death, to choose to do and say what is right even before saving his own life."

We chose God's way using sound reason and the more important truth that our wait had been ordained by God. We were not facing physical death; but in following any other way we would have not been obedient to the call of God on our lives to live fully in His will, be it waiting or moving.

Every crossroads brings a pause in the landscape of wait to look, evaluate, and make decisions as we did. Picture a crossroads in your mind. See it in the bleak, dark landscape of your wait or another's wait. Imagine yourself standing there with chin in hand and a fearful look spreading over your face. You look down each road as God asks, but you cannot see beyond your hand or beyond the next few steps. Foglike fear has descended to obscure where the road leads.

Corrie ten Boom spoke and wrote about trusting God from the perspective of her personal wait experience in a World War II concentration camp. With her father and other family members, she helped many Jews escape the Nazi Holocaust. Unwavering in her obedience to God for this saving work, Corrie was arrested with her sister Betsie and sentenced to Ravensbruck concentration camp, where eventually Betsie died. In later years Corrie ten Boom wrote, "Faith is like radar that sees through the fog—the reality of things at a distance that the human eye cannot see." When you stand at a crossroads and all you see is the fog of fear, hold on in trust to the faith God has placed within you.

Every crossroads brings opportunity to hear God's voice, but hearing requires prayer. God told Isaiah that He always hears and answers His children. "Before they call I will answer; while they are still speaking I will hear" (Isaiah 65:24). What wonderful news: God loves to converse with us about our needs. We can take comfort in talking with Him about every detail because He is listening. We can be assured He already knows the full scope of our pain, our suffering, our frustration, our sadness. We need not plead, for answers are being declared in the heavens. God's voice has spoken on our behalf!

Sometimes we will hear God's voice speaking when we listen in prayer. God's voice is described a variety of ways in Scripture. David heard God's voice booming like thunder to break in pieces the cedars of Lebanon. Elijah heard God speak with a still small voice outside the cave where he was hiding. God's voice was compelling when heard by Moses at the burning bush. God's voice was unforgettable when heard at the baptism of Jesus and recorded by Matthew, Mark, and Luke. There have moments in my life when I have heard God speak. God's voice was clear. Can I say it was audible? To me, yes! But I don't know that another in the room with me would have heard His voice speaking. I believe when God speaks to a person, He speaks directly and specifically to them alone, for He speaks His personal promise into their heart. Once you have heard God speak a promise to your heart, you will never forget that sound nor fail to recognize His voice again.

When in your landscape of wait, whether at a well or a crossroads, the invitation to talk to God and to hear His holy voice is of epic proportion. The prophet Jeremiah experienced a waiting time in jail as recorded in Jeremiah 33. In that wait, God gave Jeremiah a message for himself and for us in verse 3, "Call to me and I will answer you and tell you great and unsearchable things you do not know." *The Message* offers this: "Call to me and

I will answer you. I'll tell you marvelous and wondrous things that you could never figure out on your own." I am so thankful I do not have to figure out things on my own. When God puts you in a landscape of wait, when He leads you to a crossroads for decision making, trust this invitation and promise. God wants you to call on Him and He will not only answer, He will tell you great things, marvelous things, wondrous things.

Listening to Doubt

Every crossroads brings opportunity to obey or to disobey God. Abraham and Sarah, when they were still known as Abram and Sarai, encountered a crossroads as they entered Egypt. This story of the couple taking a wrong turn at the crossroads of decision making is found in Genesis 12:10–20.

Standing at that crossroads, they looked each way but did not ask what was the good way. Doubt filled Abraham's mind. "If" began each doubt-filled thought. "If" created a fog of fear. Should they go straight on into Egypt as husband and wife? Abraham thought if they did, he would be killed. Should they take a left turn onto the "This Is My Sister" road, what looked like a safer route? Abraham thought if they did, that his life would be spared and he would be treated well because of her. Or should they take a right turn away from Egypt altogether? Abraham knew if they took that road, they might die in the famine.

Distractions impede critical decision making. Sarah, who must have been the most stunningly beautiful woman of her time, became the distraction at their crossroads. Her beauty distracted Abraham from seeking the road God wanted them to take. They chose the "This Is My Sister" road into Egypt. Before Abraham had time to wonder where the "rest for their souls" was, Sarah's beauty was discovered and reported to Pharaoh. In an outcome worse than any of the feared ifs, Sarah was whisked off to the palace to be Pharaoh's new wife.

Corrie ten Boom, in her book *The Hiding Place*, wrote, "There are no 'ifs' in God's Kingdom. His will is our hiding place. Lord Jesus, keep me in Your will! Don't let me go mad by poking about outside it." Abraham and Sarah were poking around outside the Lord's will. God brought them together to become father and mother to His people, to be the husband and wife He would protect and prosper. There were no ifs in God's promise to them.

There are no ifs in the promises God gives to us. Any time we allow the distractions of life to cause "what if this?" to be our guide, we will miss the direction of God to journey in His will. Any time we focus on the "what if that?" doubt, we are poking around outside the Lord's will and the results are maddening.

The journey of Abraham through the landscape of wait had more crossroads than most of us will experience as we wait. There was the rescue of Lot and the destruction of Sodom and Gomorrah (Genesis 13). There was the giving of God's covenant to Abraham. There was the covenant of circumcision for all the Israelites. There was the theophany visitation and declaration of the promise of a child-to-be in one year, which we looked at in previous chapters. At all of these crossroads, God's will prevailed.

We have already looked at the crossroads decision that detoured Abraham, Sarah, and Hagar. When trust was lost in the One who had promised them they would parent a nation set aside for God, they took a drastic turn onto the wrong road. That direction led to more than a simple detour. It led to a maddening decision that caused a nation to be born that would never turn to God, a nation that would forever oppose God and His people.

Reviewing the timeline of Abraham and Sarah's journey to what would eventually become the promised land of Israel helps us see the many crossroads along their long journey of wait. When our journey of wait is prolonged with months becoming years as theirs did, we may begin to feel like the Israelites felt on their 40-year wandering in the desert, feeling as if one is moving around in circles. Even circular routes have crossroads where doubts intersect with God's will.

When on a long, circular journey of wait, we will encounter the same crossroads more than once, as did Abraham and Sarah. When entering the kingdom of Gerar (see Genesis 20), Abraham saw the continued incredible beauty of a much older Sarah, and the old fears clouded his mind. Old ifs caused Abraham to poke around again outside the Lord's will. We ask how this "sister act" could be thought as the right road to take, considering the lesson learned the hard way long ago in Egypt. Like Abraham, we poke around in old what ifs. Like Sarah we listen to old advice for old what-ifs that did not work the first time. In our humanness, we repeat the same mistakes at the same old crossroads in our wait. On the "This Is My Sister" road taken not once but twice, faithful to His promises, God protected and provided for Abraham and Sarah as He will for you.

The idea of rest for your souls is not about finding it at the end destination. It is about experiencing soul rest along the way. There were some beautiful times of rest for our souls as we waited for our home to sell in God's perfect timing. Brad and I enjoyed time together in his days of retirement and my days of working only once or twice a week. We grew even closer as we dealt with the reality of our wait and dreamed of what God had for us in the future. More visits were made with our daughter, son-in-law, and first grandchild who lived a few hours away, precious times that would help us through the longer periods of separation when the move arrived. We had added time with our friends of 30 years. Brad enjoyed one more summer and fall to play golf in his foursome on the fairways he loved at the beautiful Portsmouth Country Club. I had one more season of lunches at the Country View Restaurant with three women friends. Together we had raised our daughters from preschool through college. These times of friends spurred me to pray for God to provide new friends, to give us heart-friends wherever He would take us. We celebrated our last Thanksgiving and our last Christmas in our home with our family, making great memories of New Hampshire to hold in our hearts. We found rest for our souls, not in the destination, but throughout the journey.

APPLICATION:

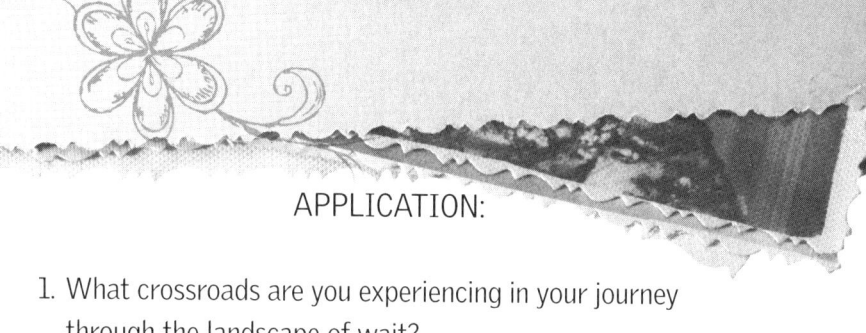

1. What crossroads are you experiencing in your journey through the landscape of wait?

2. What fog of false fear do you see at the crossroads?

3. How does the verse, "Before they call I will answer; while they are still speaking I will hear" (Isaiah 65:24), encourage you as you wait?

4. Describe the voice of God. How does God sound? What were His words to you?

5. What *ifs* have distracted you at a crossroads in your wait?

6. Where have you found rest for your soul?

CHAPTER 16

THE INTENSITY OF WAIT

THE STORY OF Rahab, a prostitute in Jericho, is one we know well from Joshua 2:1–21. We can picture the double walls of Jericho between which families lived. Our mind's eye can see Joshua's spies hiding on Rahab's roof under stalks of flax, while the king's men questioned and accused her. We can smell the fear of the city behind its closed-up gates as the stories of God's power and the Hebrew's victories melted the courage once held in pagan hearts. We can hear across history the words of Rahab's profession of faith in God, "The Lord your God is God in heaven above and on the earth below" (Joshua 2:11).

Rahab did not have the benefit of God's written Word from which to claim His promises. Rahab lived long before David played his harp or wrote his first psalm. She could not read the promise for waiting in Psalm 27:14: "Wait for the Lord; be strong and take heart and wait for the Lord." Rahab's promise from God was delivered to her by Hebrew spies, her city's enemies. But with an "Our lives for your lives!" promise, Rahab tied the scarlet cord out her window, gathered her family into the room, and, taking the cord in hand, entered a landscape of wait.

CHAPTER 16

Waiting for God's promise to be fulfilled turned out to be neither simple nor short-lived. Rahab and her family had no idea of the time frame for God's promise of protection and deliverance. Go back through chapters 2 through 6 in Joshua to see the time spans found there. For three days, Joshua's spies hid in the hills before returning to camp. For three more days, Joshua and all the Israelites camped by the Jordan River. Then came the day of a miracle-producing dry river crossing. How many days did it take for 40,000 armed men to cross the Jordan as well as all of the Israelite families? Following this crossing is the building of an altar, the celebrating of Passover, and the circumcising all the males of Israel. How many days did it take for building, celebrating, and healing? Long enough for word of Israel's approach to reach the cringing ears of the citizens of Jericho. Meanwhile, waiting in a between-the-wall room was Rahab and her family, still holding on to a scarlet cord of promise.

What thoughts came to Rahab's mind as she waited? Did arrows of doubt pierce her heart? Did courage fade even as the scarlet cord began to fade in the sunlight? Did God speak encouraging words to her, a woman He had chosen for faith and would ultimately put in the lineage of His Son Jesus?

What words were on Rahab's lips as she waited? Did she speak constant reassurances of trust in God and of the Hebrews to keep their promise? Were praises lifted up as word of the Israelites' approach finally reached her ears? Did her confession of faith in God, "The Lord your God is God in heaven above and on the earth below," become her personal litany, "The Lord my God is God in heaven above and on the earth below"?

Imagine being one of Rahab's family in that room. Suddenly you heard the marching feet of 40,000 armed warriors, the sound growing louder and louder. As the army encircled the city walls, the sound of battle-ready feet drowned out the Jericho inhabitants' cries of fear. Silence ominously returned as the army finished its single circular march. Would you have cried out, "What does this mean?" "Where is your God, Rahab?" "Do we just sit here and wait to die?" For five more days, the marching feet of God's army again arrived, circled, and left as Rahab and her family waited by the window with a life grip on the scarlet cord, their only visible hope of salvation.

You know the rest of the story. The final salvo of marching began on that seventh day. The army circled the city seven times and Scripture tells us in Joshua 6:20, "When the trumpets sounded, the people shouted, and at the sound of the trumpet, when the people gave a loud shout, the wall collapsed; so every man charged straight in, and they took the city."

Out of the rubble of the pagan city, out of the rubble of a life led for self and pleasure, and out of a wait by faith in God emerged Rahab and her family. All else perished in the battle. Days of waiting in faith, when all she had was a scarlet cord out a window and the spies' promise, were rewarded by salvation and a God-ordained future. Songwriter Don Moen presents a reading on the Integrity Music CD *God with Us* that describes the presence of Jesus in each book of the Bible. One line reads, "In Joshua He's the Scarlet thread out Rahab's window." This is a beautiful depiction of Jesus, our salvation, that we glimpse in Rahab's wait.

A lifeline of salvation is held out to all who will reach out their hands to grasp the scarlet cord of Christ's crimson blood shed for us. The gospel of Jesus brings a "My life for yours!" picture of what Jesus did on the Cross. He gave His life so our life could be saved from following pagan gods to knowing the one true God.

CHAPTER 16

He gave His life so we could be saved and emerge from the rubble of life falling down around us. He gave His life so we could be brought into the family of God and the line of Jesus by faith. It is in the intensity of wait that amazing faith emerges.

Waiting Between Life and Death

On our tenth anniversary, all the details for an evening out to celebrate were in place. Both of our parents would be arriving by late afternoon to celebrate with us. Dinner reservations were made and a special dress was hanging ready for me to wear. Ten years! The years had flown by as our child was born, our careers established, and our first home purchased.

The previous day our daughter had stepped off the bus and complained of not feeling well. A hand to her damp forehead revealed fever. As a nurse and mother, in the days before children's acetaminophen, I got out the orange children's aspirin. Fever disappeared, but nausea and vomiting started. As a professional nurse, I had always taken pride in being able to nurse my child to health through all the usual childhood sniffles, chicken pox, and scraped knees. A little tummy upset was right in the middle of my nursing and mothering skill set. But by midmorning of our anniversary, not even sips of defizzed ginger ale were staying down. Lethargy consumed our normally vibrant, talkative little girl. One of the benefits for working with family practice doctors was having direct access to them for my family. Keeping in mind our evening plans, I agreed to an ER visit to have her checked.

Our doctor was very thorough and ordered lab work. The report stunned me—Reye's syndrome. *No*, my mother's heart shouted. *God, this cannot be. No*, my nurse mind shouted. *Children die from Reye's.* Under the incredible weight of this diagnosis, my heart cried out to God for His intervention. Kim was admitted to the pediatric unit, intravenous lines were started, and an intense wait by her bedside began.

God was ahead of us in our intense need. Brad had enough help for his store so that when I called, he was out the door and on his way to the hospital to join me. My parents were already in town, having decided to leave early to have some time to relax before the celebratory dinner. They took care of feeding us and praying with us as we sat in vigil at Kim's bedside. The doctor said all we could do was wait and see as they supported her little body medically. It was an intense landscape of wait.

In those hours by her hospital bed holding her small hands in ours, I whispered over and over the name of the One who held our child in His care, "Jesus, Jesus, Jesus." I experienced the promise of God's presence for our intense time of wait. Paul's words in Romans 8:25–27 (emphasis mine) brought a sense of peace to our wait as I heard God speak the word yet to my heart.

> *"But if we hope for what we do not yet have, we wait for it patiently. In the same way, the Spirit helps us in our weakness. We do not know what we ought to pray for, but the Spirit himself intercedes for us with groans that words cannot express. And he who searches our hearts knows the mind of the Spirit, because the Spirit intercedes for the saints in accordance with God's will."*

God graciously and quickly brought healing to our child without any residual effects of the illness.

CHAPTER 16

The Bible tells us of many intense waits to assure us of His faithful presence and His sovereign will for our lives.

Abraham traveled through a three-day intense wait for God to provide a lamb as he obediently walked with his son of promise up the mountain to offer Isaac to God (Genesis 22:1–3).

It was an intense three months that Moses' parents hid their baby son in their home before setting him adrift in a basket (Hebrews 11:23).

God's people waited through the night with a hope-filled intensity behind their lamb's blood-marked doorways as their God passed over their homes, claiming the firstborn sons of the Egyptians (Exodus 12:22–23).

Esther spent three days fasting and praying as she waited to approach the king to plead for her people, the Jews (Esther 4:16).

Job's experience speaks of months of misery of a prolonged intense wait for God's intervention in his plight as he lost everything—home, children, livestock, friends, and his health.

Jesus' mother, Mary, endured exquisite emotional pain through six intense hours watching her son, her Savior, die on the Cross.

Saul, soon to be Paul, experienced the blind intensity of waiting for Jesus' promised further instructions in Damascus.

Not every wait at a bedside brings healing and recovery. Not every stricken child recovers. I recently sat with a grief counselor who ministers to parents of dying children. As she told her story of personal loss, the death of her daughter to cancer, which led her to this ministry, table conversation around us became subdued. One of the men began to speak of his loss of a son, another joined in with his story of loss of a child. The conversation was as much about the faithful presence of God in the intensity of wait as the intense pain of their loss. Not all are healed, but all who wait by faith know the grace of God for each moment in the intensity of their wait.

APPLICATION:

1. Where have you held on to the scarlet red cord in hope for the Lord?

2. Describe a time of intense wait for God's promise.

3. What verse of hope has God given you in an intense time of wait?

4. How has the Holy Spirit interceded for you when you did not have the words to pray?

CHAPTER 17

IT IS WORTH THE WAIT

THERE ARE 950 miles from our door to their door. That is the distance between my arms and the arms of our daughter, her husband, and our two grandchildren in New England. Interstate 95 is nearly a straight shot north to their home in Massachusetts on Cape Cod. We travel that highway at Christmas, our car filled with wrapped gifts to put under their tree and suitcases bulging with heavy sweaters, woolen hats, and gloves seldom worn in Myrtle Beach. Our family, in turn, travels that highway south for spring break or a week of summer vacation.

Our 11-year-old granddaughter, Megan, has inspired me to include the subject of wait being worthwhile. She recently told me, when we arrive at their house or they arrive here and pile out of their car, suddenly the months of wait and the 950-mile ride are all worth it. Someone shouts, "They are here!" We run to meet each other and hug and never want to let go. As a little one, Megan would stay nearly attached to my side for the entire visit, her arms frequently snaking up around my neck for a hug and kiss. Our grandson, Drew, now taller than me, offers a hug

CHAPTER 17

with long, gangly arms, but as a little guy, he never tired of sitting in my lap with his big *I Spy* book. We would find every item pictured on every page, again and again and again. Such delights of grandmothering.

When God first began to invite us to adventure with Him on a move south, to become involved in ministry together, the looming miles of separation were my biggest stumbling block to being on the same page as God. Everything but the distance from our daughter and her family was being resolved and finding its place in my heart and mind. Peace for long-distance grandmothering was the missing piece.

Then, while at a women's retreat at which I was leading a session on mentoring, I had an opportunity to attend a breakout session about godly grandparenting. I expected scriptural guidance and her personal advice for influencing the lives of grandchildren. Some of that was presented early on. The session leader then began to speak about long-distance grandparenting and how effective that can be in grandchildren's lives and the lives of our adult children. She spoke from personal experience with her missionary children and MK (missionary kid) grandchildren. She mentioned the technology available now to ensure staying close. But what struck me was her conviction that God would honor the obedience of grandparents who served the Lord far from their grandchildren and honor the children ministering with their children far away from family. I don't know if the session leader noticed the woman in the back row snuffling into her tissues, but God noted my tears and flooded my heart with perfect peace for the journey, adding the last piece of assurance to this extraordinary invitation to leave our home on an adventure with Him.

Choosing Doubt or Peace

God's peace is at times elusive in our journeys, journeys of going with God and journeys of waiting for God. I experienced that lack of peace in both, but discovered it in God-revealed moments. The peace to go with God came to my heart at the women's retreat. The peace to wait for God to let us go was revealed to me early one morning in my quiet-time while reading in Isaiah.

Isaiah is not an easy book of the Bible to wade through. There are the woes of God, the oracles of doom, and Isaiah's frustrations with stiff-necked people who will not heed God's denouncements through his prophecies. His messages were simultaneously for the people of that day and for people thousands of years later in a distant future. Interwoven through Isaiah's prophecies is the message of hope for Israel and for us—for unto us a child is born and unto us a Son given. Perfect hope for all peoples is prophesied as Isaiah proclaimed—He will be called Wonderful Counselor, Mighty God, Everlasting Father, Prince of Peace (see Isaiah 9:6).

That morning I was reading in Isaiah 26. Verses 3 and 4 hit me right between my spiritual eyes as I read, "You will keep in perfect peace him whose mind is steadfast, because he trusts in you. Trust in the LORD forever for the LORD, the LORD, is the Rock eternal." Continuing on, I read in verses 8 and 9, "Yes, Lord, walking in the way of your laws, we wait for you; your name and renown are the desire of our hearts. My soul yearns for you in the night; in the morning my spirit longs for you."

Isaiah tells us peace is not a quality with which we can fill ourselves. God is the giver of perfect peace. God brings His peace to those whose minds are steadfast as they trust in Him. Steadfast means without a shred of doubt. When I allowed doubts to subtly

CHAPTER 17

creep into our waiting time for God, the first thing attacked was the peace God had given in His promise to us in the first place. Ever known a doubter to be at peace over a particular issue? Doubts rob us of soul peace.

The disciple Thomas missed the first resurrected appearance by Christ to His gathered disciples. They were waiting for Jesus. The tomb was empty and now His resurrection conversations were making sense. They waited, thinking surely Jesus would come to them. Thomas, the most famous biblical doubter, has been castigated for centuries because despite excited eyewitness accounts from his brother disciples, after Jesus appeared to all of them, he wanted to see the nail-scarred hands with his own eyes. The risen Christ, appearing to the disciples said, "Peace be with you" (John 20:24–26). With his doubting, Thomas initially missed the blessed peace of belief in the Resurrection and in Jesus Christ.

Doubt robs us of the soul peace that God gives us while we wait. Doubt turns our waiting on God's promise into a search for proof that God will do what He has promised. Through sleepless nights we yearn to hear the voice of God reassuring us we are on the right road with Him. As we wake in the morning, the doubts crowd again into our mind to weaken any resolve to wait well for God. How do we stay steadfast when doubts assail our peace in God? Isaiah 26: 8–9 make it clear. We walk in the way of the Lord by staying in the Word, keeping the Lord's name on our lips in prayer, and desiring that God receive all the honor and glory of seeing His promise to us fulfilled. When steadfastness in His Word and glorifying God while waiting pushed away my doubts, perfect peace returned. Discovering the key to living life in perfect peace no matter the circumstances is worth the wait.

Doubts will also rob us of strength. Next to Isaiah 40:27 I have written, "O Debby." The words of verse 27 are personalized to now read, "Why do you say, [O Debby], and complain, [O Debby], 'My way is hidden from the Lord; my cause is disregarded by my God'?" These same thoughts Isaiah heard from God's people, were being heard from me by God. My complaints were weakening me, sapping me of the strength needed to journey through that landscape of wait.

How graciously God led me to the following verses of reminder and to God's empowering words of strength for our wait.

> *"Do you not know? Have you not heard? The Lord is the everlasting God, the Creator of the ends of the earth. He will not grow tired or weary, and his understanding no one can fathom. He gives strength to the weary and increases the power of the weak. Even youths grow tired and weary, and young men stumble and fall; but those who hope ["wait," in KJV] in the Lord will renew their strength. They will soar on wings like eagles; they will run and not grow weary, they will walk and not be faint"* (Isaiah 40:28–31).

In the vernacular of my Southern sisters, "I needed me some of that strength." I needed to exchange my doubt-driven weakness for God-renewing strength. I needed to soar above my wait to see with eagle eyes how God saw this wait. With doubts dispelled, I was strengthened to be able to run without weariness and walk without fainting in the renewed strength of the everlasting Lord. Whatever your wait, whatever your weakness, whatever the timeframe, the almighty God is standing ready to renew your strength to wait for His promise. Discovering God's strength for all your weak and weary times will be worth this wait.

Peace and strength often are cited as blessings from God—just not by me during the early days of our wait. I was thankful for God imbuing us with peace and strength, and by God's grace, these were noted by others as our wait grew long. The only thing in my mind that qualified as a blessing would be finally moving, the waiting over and the adventure beginning. If *unblessed* is a word, then there were many days that unblessed would have described my description of our wait. My Scripture search to understand waiting for God led me back to Isaiah 30:18, "Yet the Lord longs to be gracious to you; He rises to show compassion. For the Lord is a God of justice. Blessed are all who wait for Him!"

Believing in the truth of every word of Scripture, then I believed this, too, must be true even though I felt unblessed. I wrestled spiritually with my perceived dichotomy of this verse. My thinking followed these lines of internal debate. *If the Lord longs to be gracious to me, He could simply put an end to waiting and fulfill His promise immediately. If God is compassionate, He sees my agony of waiting and could act as promised, sooner not later. If God is just, then He sees how waiting is unfair, knowing we could already be serving Him in a new ministry assignment.* How quickly I protested. How quickly the Holy Spirit stopped me in my protesting tracks with the words, "Blessed are all who wait for Him!"

Yes. We want blessedness. We are hungry for His blessing. We are waiting for the very blessing He has promised. Our vision is so riveted on the end result that we have missed God's blessings along the way. The very idea that God sees us as we wait, and with us longs for the moment when He will give us what He has promised, is a blessing in itself. Because He is God, His longing is much greater than our limited human longing. God is showing His compassion. He rises from His throne in heaven to pour out compassion as He hears our every cry of frustration. He shows His compassion by extending strength to wait for His perfect timing. And because He is a just God, He blesses us with the offer of peace. Are you waiting for God? Lift up your head and count your many blessings He is providing for you. Being blessed in the wait for Him will be worth the wait.

It was most often in my lamenting to God in my quiet-time each morning that the Spirit of God would show me truths for our wait. In my search one morning for assurance that this continued waiting was indeed of God, I went to Lamentations 3:19–24. The opening words of that Scripture portion resonated with my heart. "I remember my affliction and my wandering." *Me, too, Lord*, I responded. I was Spirit-prompted to make a return journey through my quiet-time journal to revisit what God had spoken to my heart in those months. Through recorded Scriptures. meditations. and prayers, I saw the evidence of God's deep love for us. The message of God's love and compassion shone from page after page of journal entries. The depth of God's love was revealed in the landscape of wait, not in the destination of the promise; in all the blessings along the way, not in the end result. Reading on, I was struck by the bold statement in verse 22, "Because of the Lord's great love we are not consumed." The truth of this statement gave me a new promise. Not consumed did not mean I would just make it through this wait by the skin of my teeth. This meant I would no longer be fully focused on the waiting, but on the faithfulness of God. I would no longer see all of life through the lens of wait, but through the eyes of faith in the Lord who is my portion, all I needed. And this meant

CHAPTER 17

I was completely and protectively loved by the Lord in this wait for His promise. It is indeed worth the wait to know that without a shadow of doubt, "Because of the Lord's great love we are not consumed."

APPLICATION:

1. What doubts will you renounce so you can be filled with the peace of God?

2. What will you do to strengthen your resistance to the doubts that would rob you of God's peace for your wait?

3. Write out Isaiah 40:27, substituting your name for Jacob and Israel. Ask God to give you renewed strength as you wait.

4. Make a list of blessings the Lord graciously has given you in the landscape of wait.

5. How are you feeling consumed by your wait?

6. What protective love is God faithfully providing each new day?

CHAPTER 18

RENEWAL FOLLOWS WAIT

*T*HIS WAIT FOR our home to sell and to be finally on our way to the place and purpose of His promise was not life-threatening, but it was life-transforming. Our wait was not the multiple layers of critical issues some live within, waiting for God's rescue; but our wait contained multiple layers of lessons learned, presented to you in this book. In the landscape of wait for our promise of God, once we were navigating the wait in the ways of God, once we could experience the blessing of the present wait as well as the anticipated blessing of the future move, we began to hear the word *renewal* from the Lord.

The Book of Job is a chapter-by-chapter revelation of the misery of prolonged, multilayered wait. Job's incredible faithfulness in verbal response to all the ways Satan attacked him contrasts with God's silence in his insurmountable misery. His faithfulness stands out as the benchmark for high and holy waiting for God. Few of us can match this level of faithful waiting in the face of complete loss. But then, who of us have been described as Job was by God in Job 1:8, as "blameless and upright; a man who fears God and shuns evil"? Few of us have had everything stripped from our arms and from our control. Fewer have sat with our bodies oozing with sores, mourning the loss of all our children, without property or a penny to our names, and cruelly criticized by our friends; yet did not sin in what we said, as attested to in Job 2:10. In the end, after all the hard service of trust in God and 42 misery-filled chapters later, God-sized renewal came to Job.

Abraham and Sarah gave hard service of trust to God in their wait for a child and were renewed by God with the birth of Isaac 25 years after they first heard the promise. Joshua and Caleb gave hard service of trust in God for 40 years in the wilderness with Moses before entering the promised land and being renewed by God's victorious hand. Esther gave hard service of trust in God as she waited through three days of intense praying and fasting and experienced the renewal of protection, as the king's scepter was pointed her way. God's people waited in hard service of trust in the promised Messiah under the rule of pagan nations and through 400 years of silence from the last prophecy of Messiah until John the Baptist cried out, "Behold, the Lamb of God who takes away the sin of the world" (John 1:29 NASB).

As we learn the important lessons for waiting with our minds steadfast on His Word and our hearts attuned to His, we will be able to say with Job, "All the days of my hard service I will wait for my renewal to come" (Job 14:14). Renewal will come when we exit the landscape of faithful waiting and enter our promised land.

Nearly two years after first hearing God's call to leave behind family and friends, the familiar and the fulfilling, to go south to a new, not-yet-determined place to live and a new, not-yet-revealed way to minister in His name, God's promise was fulfilled. After nearly a full year's wait that took us from a level of everyday trust in God to being fully reliant on God and His will, we experienced the Holy Spirit renewal.

    Brad and I were visiting in Myrtle Beach, South Carolina, where friends had recently retired. The warm spring climate, beautiful beaches, and more than 100 golf courses welcomed us. We commented on how living along the coast could be very nice. I love days spent on the beach and Brad loves days spent on the golf course. The following morning in our quiet-time, God spoke to us from Isaiah 42:9, "See, the former things have taken place, and new things I declare; before they spring into being I announce them to you." Brad and I felt the renewal of God flood our hearts with the announcement that this was the place God had for us. With a confidence we could not attribute to any source except that of the Holy Spirit, we began our drive home with an inner knowledge that the green "go" of God was waiting for us. Before the week was out, our new realtor had an offer on our house. Within two months we were packing our belongings, saying our good-byes, and stepping out in faith to adventure with God in the next chapter of our life.

    Renewal! It is only reached at the end of the journey through God's landscape of wait. My hope for you, as you journey through your landscape of wait, is that these lessons will light the way, give you hope, and enable you to experience God's peace, joy, and strength as you wait for His promise to be fulfilled.

APPLICATION:

1. What have been the most valuable lessons learned in your hard service of waiting for God?

2. What renewal have you found as your wait has come to completion and your promise fulfilled?

3. How will you share lessons you have learned through waiting for God?

New Hope® Publishers is a division of WMU®, an international organization that challenges Christian believers to understand and be radically involved in God's mission. For more information about WMU, go to wmu.com. More information about New Hope books may be found at NewHopeDigital.com. New Hope books may be purchased at your local bookstore.

Use the QR reader on your smartphone to visit us online at NewHopeDigital.com

If you've been blessed by this book, we would like to hear your story. The publisher and author welcome your comments and suggestions at: newhopereader@wmu.org.

Resources that will restore passion for God's call on your life

Live the Call
Embrace God's Design for Your Life
WANDA LEE
ISBN-10: 1-56309-994-2
ISBN-13: 978-1-56309-994-6
N064127 • $12.99

Active Compassion
A Calling to Care
GAYLA PARKER
ISBN-10: 1-59669-314-2
ISBN-13: 978-1-59669-314-2
N124125 • $14.99

The Story Lives On
God's Power Throughout the Generations
WANDA LEE
ISBN-10: 1-59669-344-4
ISBN-13: 978-1-59669-344-9
N124149 • $14.99

Available in bookstores everywhere.
For information about these books or our authors visit NewHopeDigital.com.
Experience sample chapters, podcasts, author interviews, and more.
Download the New Hope app for your iPad, iPhone, or Android!

NEW HOPE
PUBLISHERS
Gospel-Centered. Missions-Driven.